A Bit Scott-ish

Pedalling through Scotland
in search of
Adventure, Nature
and Lemon Drizzle Cake

Mike Carden

Published by
Bike Ride Books

www.bikeridebooks.co.uk

First published in Great Britain in 2009 by Bike Ride Books

Printed in Great Britain by the MPG Books Group,
Bodmin and King's Lynn

Cover illustration and cartoons
by Robin Grenville-Evans, 2009

ISBN 978-0-9556602-1-4

Bike Ride Books
Rannerdale, 39 Market Place,
Cockermouth, Cumbria, CA13 9DP, Great Britain

A Bit Scott-ish

"Mike Carden has done it again. His combination of gentle winning humour set against some of the most powerful backdrops from Scottish history is simply a great read. Come with him on his 600-plus mile journey the length of Scotland and he'll tell you why tartan was banned (before making a very fashionable comeback), where the Holy Grail might be buried and why pasties are important to cyclists - and not just as a source of energy..."

Richard Peace, cycling journalist, creator of the Ultimate UK Cycle Route Planner and publisher of the Excellent Books range of cycling guide books.

"With beautiful and evocative descriptions of Scotland's scenery, and a superb balance of history and humour, the whole book has a lovely feel. It is just brilliant. "

Megan Taylor, author of How We Were Lost, Flame Books

"Once again we join Mike and Scott (the only bicycle that can deliver cutting one-liners) on a bracing adventure. Time to don the wet weather gear and face 'The Challenge' in Scotland. From Viking graffiti, to the Battle of Culloden, Mike tells us about it all, while taking the time to astutely remark on all the weird and wonderful people he meets on his travels. From steep highlands, to exposed moors this is the ultimate tour of Scotland told from the seat of a dry-witted bicycle held together with spare cable ties and sticky tape."

Sophie Jackson, historian and author of Churchill's Unexpected Guests

The Route

Possibly.

Beginning

Scott and I were waiting on the platform for the first of the trains that would carry us to the far northern coast. I was going to pedal back south, the length of Scotland, and it was going to be a challenge.

I was really looking forward to starting. "I almost feel I have the blood of the highlands coursing through my veins. In fact, Scott," I said, "what do you think about a kilt?"

Scott had handle-bars, a saddle, two wheels, almighty-great panniers, and a bell.

"You or me?" he said.

A lot of people have names for their bikes. A reasonable number of them talk to their bikes. Not so many get replies. Therapy had been suggested more than once, but Scott hadn't been keen.

"OK," I said. "No kilt."

I had read a little about my route. One guidebook had described a particular stretch of the ride through the Cairngorm mountains as 'a relentless and exposed climb with no shelter or facilities whatsoever for 30 kilometres'. That wasn't encouraging. I wouldn't mention it to Scott. Also, I had seen an awful weather forecast. We were going to get very wet. So perhaps, I thought, I really was here for The Challenge.

There was also the historical side. My route would go past Skara Brae, Culloden, Stirling, Bannockburn,

Edinburgh and the Borders. Names that rang with stories, and I was happy to be an amateur enthusiast.

Or maybe I was here for the natural history? It was true that nature had not always been a strong point for me by way of identification, but I had opened a couple of books on the subject and I could possibly become an amateur enthusiast. Perhaps I would see red deer and roe deer, golden eagles and white-tailed eagles, puffins and ptarmigans. Or maybe red grouse and black grouse, penguins and polar bears, grizzly bears and wolves, although I was conscious that some of those were less likely than others.

'The next train,' came the announcement over the tannoy, 'is the 10.54 to Edinburgh.'

Then of course, there was the Mid-Life Crisis.

I had decided at the end of my last long journey, cycling from one end of England to the other, that perhaps what the ride had really been about was a serious case of Mid-Life Crisis. Maybe the choice had been cycling off with Scott or buying a fast, red sports car. I had intended to find the solution to Mid-Life, the Universe and Everything. The problem was that I had reached the border with Scotland and never did find that solution. Perhaps this next journey would do it. Either that or Scott would drive me bananas.

"Scott", I said. "We are going to be cycling up a relentless and exposed climb with no shelter or facilities whatsoever for 30 kilometres. We are going to visit castles and see grizzly bears, and one of us might have a Mid-Life Crisis."

"Just tell me again that neither of us will be wearing a kilt."

As the trains took me north, the atmosphere gradually changed. From the border at Carlisle as far as Edinburgh, there had been the usual mix of travellers for work and pleasure. But standing at the station at Edinburgh, it felt like the start of a journey. I was early, and though the train was already at the platform, the doors were still locked. I wheeled

Scott along until we found a carriage with a cycle sign, and we waited. After a few minutes, a younger guy wheeled his bike along towards me, panniers hanging off his bike as well.

"This is it," I said, and I nodded to the cycle sign on side of the train.

"Thanks," he said.

He was about thirty, lean, with friendly blue eyes, and he was going to cycle from John O'Groats to Lands End. "It's for charity," he said. "My mother died two years ago, and I'm raising money for the British Heart Foundation."

"Oh. I'm sorry."

"And you? Why are you cycling?"

"It's The Challenge."

"Right."

"Well, Scott and me - "

"Scott?"

I indicated my two-wheeled companion with '*SCOTT*' written in large letters on one of his tubes.

"Ah. Scott."

"And I'm Mike," I said.

"Niall."

We shook hands. "Scott and me, we like a challenge."

Niall and I chained Scott and Niall's (unnamed) bike together in the section of the train set aside for cycles, and sat opposite each other.

The train began to fill up, with groups of women struggling to find their seats. Some had Scots flags emblazoned on their T-shirts, all had smiles on their faces. I had a suspicion that some of those smiles had been encouraged by a liquid lunch in Edinburgh, and that festivities had been renewed. A lady with the blue-white cross of St Andrew straddling her front stopped by my table.

"Can I ask," I said, "what's happening?"

"It's the Women's Tartan Army. We're all on our way to Aviemore for the weekend. We did it before when Scotland didn't get into the European Championships, and it was better than going to a match."

"I bet."

"So we're all doing it again."

She lurched on down the train. Four cheery ladies sitting opposite had been listening in.

"Are you in the Tartan Army as well?" I asked.

"No," one said. "We're going on a hen weekend to Inverness." She grinned a slightly lop-sided grin.

I exchanged a look with Niall. We were outnumbered.

Niall was from Leeds, a civil engineer responsible for rail bridges for his company. Within just a few minutes of leaving Waverley Station in Edinburgh, we were trundling across the Forth Rail Bridge. Niall craned his head trying to look out both train windows at the same time, as the stately columns flowed past us.

A short distance away, the towers of the Forth Road Bridge stood tall, and I admired its shape.

Niall had no interest. "It's just a road bridge."

Beyond the wide Firth of Forth, Fife looked pretty, and the rail line took us past low green hills and blue stretches of water.

"So what route are you taking?" Niall asked.

"I'm getting the train to Thurso, the ferry from there to the Orkney Islands, cycling across the main island, then taking the ferry to John O'Groats and zig-zagging down through Scotland to the border."

I got out my maps and we compared routes. His route was A-roads. 70 miles a day. A fast and furious journey, hardly stopping, except to camp at night. Mine scrupulously avoided A-roads, except for A-roads in Orkney and the far north of Scotland, where that might well be the only way through mountains. Mostly I would be on country lanes, B-roads or cycle lanes – with any luck.

I had puzzled for some while over what route I would take through Scotland. I could have cycled around the Western Isles. Or all down the East coast on National Cycle

Route 1. But if I went down the centre, I found by studying the map, I could go to the places that arguably had made the Scots: in Orkney I could see prehistory and Vikings; in the far north there would be the Clearances of the 19th century, with men and women driven from their homes to the mills of the south or across the sea to America or Australia; from Inverness there would be Culloden and Bonnie Prince Charlie's doomed fight for the crown supported by the clans; then out of the highlands to Stirling and Bannockburn, where William Wallace and then Robert the Bruce had fought for Scotland's independence from England.

From there I would cut across to Fife, and that was where my own history was leading me. I had lived in Fife from the age of two months to the age of seven, an English boy with a Scottish accent – and socks always up to my knees. Was it possible that I was going home?

Then to Edinburgh and over the southern uplands through wool and mill country, with many mills now standing empty, before sliding south to finish at the border. That was the plan.

Altogether I guessed that the route would be over 500 miles (800 kilometres). I planned to do the journey in fourteen days, and had booked accommodation all the way. If I didn't make a day's journey, I would have nowhere to stay.

Beyond Perth the train entered real hill country. Through Pitlochry and we were in the highlands themselves. Mountains began to rear either side. Proper ones, with high rugged peaks. Some even had patches of snow in crevices towards the summits. The end of June, and there was snow lying. The Adventure, I thought. I'm doing this for the Adventure.

Just before Aviemore, one of the Tartan Army ladies reappeared to queue for the loo, its door just back from our table. Blonde, flushed of face and similarly T-shirted to her friend, she turned when a voice called to her, "You don't have time."

"I've got to," she shouted back, her be-flagged chest jiggling as she crossed and uncrossed her legs.

A middle-aged man in a suit was already standing waiting. "I'm sorry," he said to her, a distinct lack of sympathy in his voice, "but I was here first."

"Ooh."

The entire half of the carriage was watching as the occupant of the toilet departed and suit-man went in.

"You don't have time," a voice called. "We're nearly there."

Jiggle. "I've really got to."

"We're getting off."

"Ooooh." Jiggle, jiggle.

The man finally left and she dived through the door.

Two tartan army ladies in their proud T-shirts crept up to the door, smirking. "Aviemore," one said, deepening her voice. "This is Aviemore."

"Quick," said the other. "We're here."

The toilet door opened and a relieved face poked through.

"I hate you," she said, grinning.

Beyond Aviemore the mountains and moorland seemed to go on forever. Vast empty boggy spaces alongside the track, then heather moors rising up to rugged peaks and those scary little patches of white at the tops.

There were sheep. The odd few cows. And a lonely cyclist on the nearby cycle track heading north. My rail journey north would be very similar to some of my cycle route south. I pointed out the track to Niall.

"I'll be there," I said, and it came home to me just how high and exposed the route looked from the warm train.

From a fence post, an owl glided alongside for a few moments and was gone. I think it was an owl anyway.

The train on from Inverness was different again. It was the evening train, finishing at Thurso on the north coast, my destination, and then reversing back to Wick on the north-east coast.

There was a young Scotsman in a kilt, who strode jauntily up the corridor.

There were walkers in muddy boots – a young Norwegian couple.

"Yess," he said. "We walk." And he showed me what walking meant with his fingers.

Diagonally opposite us sat another young couple, a six-pack of lagers on the table in front of them. The man appeared to be reasonably thirsty, though it wasn't too long before he was snoring benignly on his girlfriend's shoulder. Occasionally, she moved his head off to take a small nip herself, or to offer a can to the girl opposite her. This girl was young and blonde, with a wonderful accent; definitely Scots, but not an accent I was familiar with.

The train followed the coast for some way, and it was beautiful. Out of the window was just grass, then a dry stone wall, then sand, then a blue sea. Totally different to the mountains I had been through so far. It was absolutely magnificent.

When the couple poured themselves off the train, and our course took to moorland on its way north, the young blonde turned to Niall and myself. Well, mostly Niall, who had a slight age advantage on me.

"What are you two doing?"

"Cycling," Niall said.

"Reeally? Where?"

"Well, I'm cycling from John O'Groats to Land's End."

"Reeally? Oh."

I said, "And I'm going to Thurso and Orkney and then back down through Scotland."

"Are you not together then?"

"No," I said. "We just met on the station at Edinburgh."

"Oh, I thought you were his Dad."

This stumped me for a short while, and she chatted with Niall. When she turned back to me she said, "Why would you want to do all that cycling?"

"It's Mid-life Crisis," I said.

"Oh."

Her attention wandered to the window. "Ooh. Deers. Look," she said, turning back to Niall. "Deers."

And there were. A herd of red deer were grazing just beyond a tall fence next to the line. Some with antlers, others without. Heads down and grazing, or watching our train make its stately way across the tussocky moorland.

She got out her phone. "Hey, it's Jen," she said. "I just had to phone and tell you. There are deers. What? Deers. Yes. Lots of them. Just out the window."

She listened for a while.

"No. There's more than one. Deers."

I tuned out, gazing at the moorland jogging past. It occurred to me that this piece of Scotland looked no distance on the (foreshortened) TV weather forecast, but on the ground had become a four-hour train journey.

"Bye then," she said into her phone and she turned her attention back to Niall. "Where are you from?"

"Leeds."

"I know some people from Leeds. Moved to Thurso. Can't think why. It's boring."

"Where are you from?" I asked her.

"Thurso. It's boring. There's nothing to do."

"Is that why you were in Inverness?"

"I was visiting a friend who's moved there. Are you staying in Thurso?"

"Just one night."

"That's good. Because it's reeally boring. I'm moving away when I finish college."

"What are you studying?"

"Hairdressing. There's only two things you can study in Thurso. Hairdressing and game-keeping. Ooh look. Deers."

Which left me with an extraordinarily vivid mental picture of Thurso teeming with young game-keepers sporting the most up-to-date hairstyles imaginable.

Towards ten o'clock the train began to pull in to Thurso. I moved back to fix my panniers on to Scott.

"Vott iss zis?"

I had a young German lad beside me examining the interesting arrangement above Scott's back wheel of mud guard, pannier-carrier, sticky tape and cable ties, those little strips of plastic that are designed to pull tight round cables and stay there. More than once, something had come unscrewed or had fallen off. In fact, I reflected, parts of Scott were permanently held together by cable ties.

It could have been 'mechanical blindness'. Perhaps it wasn't that; perhaps I was mechanically-challenged? There ought to be a technical term, anyway, for the inability to absorb how to mend anything mechanical. I had mended the odd thing on Scott, but each time it seemed almost accidental, and afterwards my mind seemed to blank out what steps I had taken. If I did have to mend something for a second time, I was none the wiser about where to start. Unless of course it involved sticky tape and cable ties.

That's one of the reasons why Scott and I seemed to get on together. He rarely seemed to need mending. OK, he was a bit long in the tooth, and considerably slower than a slick new touring bike. But he had rarely let me down.

I kept a full tool kit with me, but to be honest, I wouldn't have had the foggiest what to do with, for example, a chain-tool-thingie.

I could change tyres. I had regularly changed tyres. But I'd have rather not. So when my local bike shop had suggested Kevlar-lined tyres, I'd jumped at it.

"Kevlar? As in 'bullet-proof'?"

"Yup."

"Wow. So if I am ambushed by kidnappers with loaded sawn-off shotguns pointed at me, I can whip off my Kevlar-lined tyres and hide behind them?"

"Pardon?"

"So they're good for stopping punctures then?"

Scott now had two Kevlar-lined tyres on, and I was pretty confident in them. Even so, it occurred to me that I had forgotten to add a spare inner tube to my otherwise mystifying took kit. And I had forgotten that main stand-by of mine over the years: spare cable ties.

I knew what to do with cable ties.

The German lad was still examining Scott's arrangement above the back wheel.

"It works," I said.

"Oh."

I'm not sure he was very impressed.

It does work though.

"You ride verr?"

"From here to the border. With England."

He looked at me.

"It's The Nature," I said. "Deers. Wolves. Grizzly bears. That sort of thing."

As I turned Scott round to wheel him into the doorway, Niall came to join me.

"You know you said there's a ferry to Orkney from John O'Groats. Well, I might just join you."

"You're going south."

"I've some spare time before I head back to work. I'll text you in the morning."

"Great." Niall would be good company.

I followed Jen off the train.

"Do you know where you're going?" she asked.

"Yes, I'm fine, thank you." And I pulled my directions from my pocket.

So she smiled and wished me a good ride. A young boy cycled up to her, and brother and sister disappeared into the town, giggling together. I looked around for game-keepers with very smart hair, but didn't spot any, and then I got lost when I cycled out of the station.

I had followed the instructions I had been given, turning left then right. Before I knew it, I had passed Tescos, climbed a hill, and I was cycling out of the town.

"This can't be right," I said to Scott. I phoned for more directions and cycled back almost to where I had started from.

My hosts at the guest house were a couple of retirement age, and my room was chintz and comfortable. Leaving my bags, we pedalled down to the harbour. Beyond the harbour wall, low waves rolled in over a beach of wet sand, stones and seaweed. It was not really a sand-castle-making beach, more of a surfing beach, with Thurso voted a top ten surfing beach in Europe, and one of the homes of the world championships. That didn't sound too boring. In fact, it was rather surprising.

It was nearly ten o'clock in the evening, but warm, with puffy white clouds beginning to tinge pink from a sun setting behind the headland of the bay. I phoned home and described to Claire the show going on in the heavens. As we talked, the clouds turned from rose pink to amber, and then to gold. Gaps of sky became Mediterranean blue and the gold flowed into rivers of boiling molten lava. Mount Etna was exploding above my head.

I pushed Scott down the slipway, dipping his front wheel in a wave as it spread towards us. To the north, across a short few miles of sea, the cliffs of the Orkney Isles were a darkening blue.

Yesterday, some hundreds of miles from here, I had watched that wet weather forecast and wondered why I was *really* going to spend the next two weeks on a journey across Scotland with a recalcitrant bicycle.

Now it was suddenly clear. Not that I could explain it quite yet.

"Scott," I said. "I think I know why we're here."

"Good," he said. "Can we go home now?"

Part One

The Orkney Islands
to Inverness

Day One

Target: 31 miles / 50 Km
from Thurso to Kirkwall, Orkney
via Stromness and Skara Brae

The Orkney Islands

Birsay

West Mainland

Skara Brae

Stones of
Stenness

Finstown

Ring of
Brodgar

Maeshowe

Kirkwall

East
Mainland

Stromness

Isle of
Hoy

I sent a text to Niall as I ate breakfast. "Which way are you going? North or South?"

The reply was almost instant. "Definitely North."

He wouldn't be on my early ferry from Scrabster, just around the bay from Thurso. Niall had been staying at Wick on the east coast, so his closest ferry would be near John O'Groats, a ferry that would drop him at the other end of the islands. Or he would have to cycle even further to Scrabster to catch me up.

As I loaded the panniers on to Scott outside the kitchen door, the word for today's weather came to me. It was 'dreich'. I think that was the word anyway. I had lived in Scotland until I was seven, and 'dreich' popped into my head. Low, murky clouds. The threat of rain. 'Dreich'.

Thurso was quiet on this dreich Saturday morning as I cycled around to the far side of the bay towards Scrabster. The harbour sat under cliffs, and as I approached, a yellow-and-orange ship in the port grew larger and larger. 'Subsea Viking' was the name on the side.

"That's it, Scott, we're going on a submarine."

Five stories high, with a giant crane at one end, a helicopter pad at the other, and orange lifeboats hanging off the side, it actually looked very unlike anything that might go subsea.

A security man waved me past waiting cars and I gestured to Subsea Viking. "What is it?"

"Tests the seabed. Oil and so on," he said, then turned his back.

"Right. Thanks."

The rain came on, and I went into the quiet terminal building for my ticket. When I came out, the cars were driving down the ramp on to the ferry, a slightly less substantial ship than Subsea Viking. No helicopter pad anyway.

When they were on board and parked, I cycled alone down the ramp into the bowels of the ship and it felt like the start of something. An adventure? Well, maybe.

The ferry was new-ish and looked-after, the roll in the

swell was gentle, and I settled in by a window and dozed off. When I looked up after an hour, the cliffs of the first Orkney island, Hoy, were looming through drifts of misty cloud. And there was the highest sea-stack I had seen. The Old Man of Hoy, a tall and narrow pillar of dark rock, standing proud from the sea below, a lone figure holding out against the waves. With wisps of cloud blowing past, this was like The Lost World.

I went out on deck to take in the broad spread of The Lost World, and the cliffs were surprisingly close, with The Old Man lurking in front. In the worsening rain, two older ladies had cameras with long lenses focused on those high rock walls and on the sea-birds wheeling through the mist above the waves.

The ferry followed the cliffs around to the north, where an inlet appeared, and we steamed through. To the left was a lower island – Mainland – green and gentle compared to the wilds of Hoy across on the right. The name 'Mainland' was the flimsy excuse for being on Orkney at all. I had originally decided to cycle from one end of mainland Scotland to the other, but had found that not only was Orkney a short ferry ride away, but that the largest island was called Mainland. No choice really.

Low houses appeared on Mainland and coalesced into the town of Stromness, strung along the sea front. The ferry docked, and I went down to find Scott amongst the cars. We pedalled off last and followed signs into the town.

A narrow paved road wiggled through old houses and shops. The buildings on the left had gardens or yards shelving down to the water. Those on the right had steep alleyways and steps climbing the hill behind, including the intriguing 'Khyber Pass'.

We made our way slowly through the rain, avoiding pedestrians and cars sharing the twisting main street. It became clear that Stromness had some history. One building bore a blue plaque: 'The Haven. Agents of the Hudson Bay

Company operated from this house and signed many Orcadians into company service'. Another said: 'Mrs Humphrey's House. Temporary Hospital 1835 – 1836 for scurvy ridden whale men who had been trapped in the ice for months'. And then a stone, almost like a gravestone, but marking the spot of an old well: 'There watered here The Hudson Bay Company's ships 1670 – 1891, Captain Cooke's vessels Discovery and Resolution, Sir John Franklin's ships Erebus and Terror on Arctic exploration 1845'.

I had a text from Niall.

"Missed ferry at John O'Groats. Cycling to Scrabster. With you 1.30."

"Fine," I replied. "See you then."

I had a couple of hours to kill.

In Stromness museum an English voice greeted me and I was curious.

"That's not an Orkney accent."

"No, it's definitely an English accent."

He was around my age, a long way from where he had gained his accent, welcoming visitors to the town museum in Stromness.

"Can I ask, how is it you're here?"

"Oh, I came here on holiday in 1988 and fell in love with the island. In fact I decided almost at once that I wanted to move here and started getting the local newspaper sent to me. It took another ten years to actually move, but, well, here I am."

"That's wonderful," I said, and I meant it. I'd been on the island around fifteen minutes, and I could see that the place could cast a spell.

The best parts of the museum were those concentrating on Orkney's exploring past. Orcadians had hunted for the North West Passage through Canada to the Far East and they had searched for the source of the Niger. They had been prized by the Hudson Bay Company in Canada as the hardest of their workers, trading for furs and pelts with the natives. Some

Orcadians settled and took wives, and there were records of the son of one union who went to school in Stromness before going back to join his mother's tribe. It was all fascinating.

"Scott," I said, outside in the drizzle, putting my waterproof jacket on. "This is an island for real men. For explorers. For discoverers of lost worlds."

"And that relates to you how?"

"I'm going to journey into the unknown. To boldly go where no man has gone before." Silence from Scott. "That sort of thing."

We cycled up out of the town on the main road, cars swishing past in rain which was becoming steadily heavier. After about four miles, passing green cow-fields and lone houses, a bus shelter appeared. The shelter had glass sides most of the way around, so I wheeled Scott in for some respite from the rain.

"I could do with overtrousers on, Scott," I said.

"Oh yes, very discoverer of lost worlds."

I put the full kit on. Overtrousers. Overshoes. Waterproof cover for my helmet. Not much of me remained open to the elements. In the past, with a yellow jacket, yellow pannier covers and a black helmet cover, the word 'banana' had been mentioned. My new jacket was a pale blue, and any mention of 'that banana on a bike' I knew would not refer to the colour of my jacket.

"And you can keep quiet," I said.

Before long we were turning off, on a single-track lane following signs for 'Route 1' into a World Heritage Site, which would include a burial mound, two stone circles and a stone-age village.

Route 1 is a cycle route built by the good people of Sustrans, the cycling charity. Sustrans have around 15,000 miles of waymarked cycle routes either in place or in the process of being built or signposted. I even had a Sustrans map: one which should lead me around Mainland Orkney, over to John O'Groats, then by devious means down to

Inverness, where I would switch to a new Sustrans map. Some of Sustrans' routes are off-road cycle lanes. Others, such as where I was, are quiet country lanes, marked by little blue and red Sustrans signs.

We missed the burial mound. I'm not sure how. I'd been looking forward to it as well. Maeshowe. In my head I pronounced it 'Mice, How?', but I gathered the local pronunciation was mezzhoo.

Maeshowe was 5,000 years old, with an entrance passage aligned so that the sun shone right to the end on mid winter's day. There was also Viking graffiti such as, 'These runes were carved by the man most skilled in runes in the western ocean with this axe owned by Gauk Trandilsson in the South land'. Good stuff.

Anyway, I must have had the rain in my eyes, or been watching out for The Stones of Stenness, but either way, I missed it.

The Stones of Stenness were enormous. Just four of them were left, so far as I could see. Big slabs of grey rock, fairly narrow but several metres high and sliced off diagonally at the top. They were pretty impressive.

I left Scott by the stile and climbed through for a better look. A sheep was guarding one, and I took out the camera, taking a long-distance shot. I crept closer. The sheep would give the picture scale, I thought. Closer. Camera up. "Smile," I said, and it fled.

My phone buzzed with a text from Niall.

"Missed ferry at Thurso. Cycling back to ferry at John O'Groats."

"Right-o."

The Stones of Stenness sounded like they were straight out of The Lord of the Rings, as did The Ring of Brodgar, somewhere ahead of me.

The lane became a causeway with stretches of water either side, and I was unsure if they were sea inlets or freshwater lakes. A gentle hill came up on the left, with standing stones visible on top. I left Scott by the road and followed a lady up the slope to The Ring of Brodgar. The stones were slightly smaller than at Stenness, but there were many more of them, placed in a vast circle amidst heather and long grasses. With the land falling away on either side and the rain easing, this was a fantastic place. It was very atmospheric – the water, the lurking low cloud, and the great standing stones.

"Wonderful, isn't it?" I said.

"Yes."

"Are you here on holiday?"

"My daughter bought my husband and me a long weekend in Orkney. We've come up from Glasgow."

I looked around. She did appear to be by herself, but I decided not to mention that.

"So are you both enjoying Orkney?"

"Ye-es. Shame about the rain."

"Mm."

As we walked back down the hill, a car appeared and tooted its horn. She got in.

"Bye," I said.

And they drove off.

Well, I was enjoying the place.

As I reached Scott back at the road, a coach party arrived. I had timed my visit well.

Another few miles of cycling through pleasant green countryside, and we were at one of the main targets of my journey, Skara Brae.

In 1850 a huge storm blew much of the sand dunes away from the coast at Skaill Bay on the west coast of Mainland. This revealed the sunken remains of a stone age village – almost intact. I had seen photos, and it seemed like it would be an amazing place.

Leaving Scott out front, I scented a café.

"I plan to have lemon drizzle cake, Scott. You have to really."

"Have to?"

"Part of my five a day."

Silence from Scott.

"Five portions of fruit or vegetables a day. That's what they say."

"Lemon drizzle cake?"

"Yes," I said. "For the Vitamin C."

"So how much Vitamin C is there in lemon drizzle cake?"

"I'll ask for an extra-large portion."

The visitor centre was warm and welcoming, and I ordered a cup of tea. They didn't have lemon drizzle cake.

"Flapjack please," I said.

Beyond the visitor centre is a reconstruction of one of the stone-age houses. The originals were dug down into giant rubbish heaps – almost like building your house in a compost heap. The insulation must have been tremendous. Lined with dry-stone walling, and domed over the top, it was reasonably spacious. But what grabbed the attention was the 'furniture'. There was a dresser of stone, complete with shelves, plus a bed with stone-slabs at the sides, and a fire. And in this reconstruction, there were reconstructed plastic lobsters waiting on top of the dresser for the fire to warm up. Fred Flintstone would have been perfectly happy here.

I ducked through a low doorway and then followed the path down to the bay and to the original houses set deep in their grass-covered compost, overlooking the sea. There must have been around twenty people mooching around the little site. It felt busy.

The path twisted its way at grass level, so that you could look down from roof height into half a dozen of these hobbit-like, little, round houses. Extraordinarily, they all had similar designs. The stone dresser, stone beds and stone fireplaces almost identical from one to another. As if the inhabitants had been to a stone-age IKEA and bought a job lot. But this was 5,000 years ago, before the pyramids were built, and these were stone-age people with only a thin understanding of the notion of flat-pack furniture.

"It's an astonishing place," I said to a Historic Scotland lady in her blue uniform.

"It is," she said. She gestured at the curve of beach below, rounding off at a rocky headland. "And it's a lovely place to work."

"The accent," I said, noting another non-local I had come across. "It's not Scottish."

"No," she laughed. "I'm originally from Cheshire. But it's really good here."

I was beginning to suspect this might become a theme.

Back with Scott, I checked my map. I had cycled twelve miles since Stromness. Not too far at all, but with the ferry journey and my stops, it was already getting on in the day. If I continued on Route 1, I would do long loops around Mainland and it would take me another 40 miles to get to my bed for the night at Kirkwall Youth Hostel. Too far. If I went the quickest route, I guessed it would be about 20 miles. I decided to compromise. I would cycle up to the furthest north point of Mainland, but then go as direct as possible to Kirkwall. Maybe another 30 miles. Still a long way for a man of doubtful fitness on the first day of the ride, but the sun was out, I felt good, and of course Orkney is known for its flatness.

We set off north and I decided to make conversation.

"Scott," I said. "They didn't have any lemon drizzle cake."

"I expect Captain Cooke had the same problem," he said.

"I may get scurvy."

There were hills north of Skara Brae. They were not big hills. But they were hills, and I became increasingly conscious that I was still cycling away from Kirkwall.

The country was grand though. Grassy fields of cows and buttercups dropping away to a now-blue sea. Marshy spots by the road with yellow irises. In fact quite a lot of marshy spots with yellow irises. And hay fields either waiting to be cut or just-cut. Where they had been cut, the fields sprouted all manner of long-beaked birds, pottering around and jabbing at the ground. Especially common were the black-and-white birds with red, pointy beaks, which my mind dredged up as oyster-catchers. They looked like they had been constructed on a painting-by-numbers board, hard edges of black and white, and that sharp, red, unreal beak.

Occasional low white bungalows sat next to the road, windows looking out to sea, with well-tended gardens full of flowers. They seemed to say that the owners loved this place and were looking after it.

When I got to a point where I could drop down to the coast at Birsay on the north west corner of the island, I hesitated.

Below me on the coast were the remains of sites built by the Picts and the Vikings. The Picts were given that name by the Romans when they invaded Scotland. Picts comes from 'pictii' – the 'painted people'. The 'Scots' came later, invading (confusingly) from Ireland. Spreading east, the Scots had come into conflict with the Picts, but what brought an end to the Pictish kingdoms was the arrival of the Norsemen – the Vikings in their long boats. The Orkney Islands, the Shetland Islands, the Western Isles and much of the far north of Scotland were raided and then settled by Norsemen. The Orkney Islands only became part of the Kingdom of Scots in the fifteenth century.

So, before a big move to Kirkwall by the Norsemen, this little corner of land had been the main settlement in Orkney. I could also see the sixteenth century Earl's Palace down there.

That's why I hesitated.

But Kirkwall was still about 25 miles away as the bike rides, and the afternoon was on me. I could feel a chill breeze and realised that some grey clouds were also on me.

"Onwards," I said to Scott.

We were on an A-road now, but it didn't feel like one. It was quiet, with views out along the north coast. The hills were getting harder, but maybe that was because my legs had already cycled 20 miles or so. The rain started, and was suddenly heavy. It hadn't really occurred to me until now how little shelter there was. There were no trees at all. More importantly, there were no cafés and I still hadn't had my lemon drizzle cake. I was probably suffering from a Vitamin C deficiency. I put on my full waterproof kit.

A loch came into view on my right, which my map told me meant that the most northerly point of Mainland Orkney was on my left. We stopped and I looked north at grey sea for any sign of seals, dolphins or whales. Nothing. Just, well, grey sea.

"From now on, Scott, we go south. We go in search of Adventure, Nature, and Lemon Drizzle Cake. Though not necessarily in that order."

Actually, it was more south-east-ish that we were heading, with the rain from one side, and mist and cloud ahead. Finally some trees loomed, standing guard around a house. As I stopped for a rest under what meagre shelter they gave and for a chocolate biscuit, my back mudguard fell off. Mending it involved getting at my toolkit, not too handily placed at the bottom of a pannier. As the rain dripped through the trees, I stood over the pannier to pull out bags of clothes, maps and books in order to get at the toolkit. Sunshine and views of the sea had gone. This was really quite unpleasant.

I looked at the map. I still had a very long way to go, even staying on the main road.

I had not heard from Niall and sent him a text. "Where are you?"

No reply came through. There was an outside chance he had missed his ferry. In this weather, I was beginning to wish I had missed my ferry. My legs were certainly telling me they had gone quite far enough for a first day. But there was nowhere to stop. There was no choice. I had to plough on.

At Finstown came the first sign of somewhere I might stop for a break and some refreshment. I wanted to stop. Forty-odd miles done on my first day, and this relentless rain.

I was very tired. But by then I was about five flat-ish miles from Kirkwall, and I decided to press on. I really just wanted to be there.

As we cycled into Kirkwall, the rain disappeared, the clouds blew away as suddenly as they had come, and my legs recovered some life. I found myself at the harbour and marina, with signs for sailings to Shetland and to Aberdeen, and with sunshine drying the roads and pavements.

"Excuse me," I said to a man coming out of a bar. "Can you tell me where the Youth Hostel is?"

"Yes. Of course. Left here. Keep going straight." That had to be an Orkney accent. Not at all like Glasgow or Edinburgh, but then Norse roots go deep in Orkney. "Then a right fork, up the hill, and down on the left."

"Thank you."

Surprisingly, I found it.

Kirkwall Youth Hostel was a flat-roofed set of buildings, neither old nor new, maybe in need of some money spent on it, but seemingly friendly. After all, when the warden saw me wheel Scott around to the door, he immediately exclaimed, "A 'Purgatory'!" and his eyes lit up.

Now, Scott may be a 'Scott', but on the side of the frame is also written '*Purgatory*', an interesting marketing ploy for a cycle manufacturer. I had often wondered if they had other similar names for bikes – '*Hell*" perhaps.

I agreed that Scott was indeed a '*Purgatory*'.

The warden walked around him. "I almost bought a 'Purgatory'." He shook his head, clearly moved by the memory.

"Oh. Right," I said.

He stifled a sniff, and I suspect was trying not to wipe away a tear.

In my many years accompanying Scott on his travels, I had never yet seen him cause such emotion.

"Well… yes… right," I said.

He dragged his eyes away from Scott. "I'll, um, book you

in then, shall I?"

I decided that this new business-like demeanour was a cover. As he went inside, I lifted my panniers from Scott.

"Do you realise," Scott said, "that I am almost legendary on Orkney?"

"Almost," I said.

I sent a text to Niall: "At Kirkwall Youth Hostel. Did you make it?"

"Sorry," he replied. "Missed the ferry. Think I had better head south tomorrow. Good luck."

I wasn't entirely surprised.

I was given a sheet sleeping bag and a key, and found my way to a dormitory with two sets of double bunks. Both bottom beds were already taken, although their occupants weren't there.

One guy had strewn carrier bags and a rucksack across his bed. The other had hung several neatly ironed shirts and a suit on hangers from the top bunk's rail, and underneath the bed was a pair of highly polished black shoes and a briefcase. I suspected that the two of them were not together.

I chose the bunk above 'Guy One', and stood half-way up the ladder to wrestle my sheet sleeping bag into place. Never the best start to staying in a hostel, but then, hostels are such great value, and of course you talk to people, which you wouldn't either in a hotel or in a tent. You also, unfortunately, have to put up with snoring and any other unpleasant nightly habits, but then, if we're honest, so do they.

Guy One appeared before long. He was of a good age, bald in the middle of his head, with long, non-matching tufts of hair on either side of his head. He also had a slightly disreputable jumper.

"'Ello," he said. London accent.

"Hi. Are you here on holiday?" I asked.

"Yes, 'ere for a week, going to the islands on the ferries. Come every year. Fantastic place. Birds. People. Fantastic."

The door opened and Guy Two came in.

Guy One ignored him.

Guy Two was a smart man in tie, jacket and trousers, but it was the hair that you noticed first, silver and shoulder length.

"Hello," he said. BBC English.

"And are you here on holiday as well?"

"No. Conference."

"Right," I said. "Do either of you know of somewhere I could eat?"

I was by now starving.

"Fish and chip shop down the road," said Guy Two.

Guy One ignored him and me.

"Good."

The hostel was a rabbit-warren of rooms. Twelve dormitories, a large dining area and kitchen, a lounge, showers and bathrooms. Importantly, there was also a warm drying-room. I washed out clothes and hung them and my soggy trainers from washing lines trailed across the room. I was not the only one to get a soaking that day.

In dry non-cycling clothes, I fetched Scott and we pedalled down to the fish and chip shop. On a bench still damp from the rain, I had my fish and chips as the good lads and lasses of Kirkwall made their way into town.

I still hadn't had my lemon drizzle cake of course. I would have to make sure that I had my five-a-day tomorrow.

Captain's log: Day One

Target for the day:	31.0 miles	49.6 Km
	(a sensible distance)	
Actual distance:	46.1 miles	73.8 Km
	(ridiculous for a first day)	
Average speed:	10.1 mph	16.2 Kmph
	(very slow)	
Maximum speed:	32.0 mph	51.2 Kmph
	(downhill, wind behind me)	
Vitamin C Deficiency:	off the scale	

I was asleep when Guy Three came in during the night. He was extraordinarily noisy. I could put up with him bumping into things in the dark, but I wasn't so keen on the tube-clearing. Then he sneezed violently. Twice. I checked my watch. 4.15am.

Not good.

Eventually, he settled.

I was just getting back to sleep when the snoring started.

It's the Adventure, I thought.

Day Two

**Target: 22 miles / 35 Km
from Kirkwall, Orkney to John O'Groats
via the Italian Chapel**

Guy Two was gone when I woke up. It was Sunday morning, so a conference was unlikely, but you never know. I leaned over the side of the bunk to check on Guy One, and he was sound asleep. Guy Three was stirring though, and I broke into action. If there is one thing that would get me out of bed in the morning, it would be the determination not to be around when the morning tube-clearing started.

I dressed quickly and made my way along to the kitchen with a bag containing my remaining food from yesterday. Coffee, muesli bar and fruit cake inside me, I picked up my clothing and trainers from the drying room. They were still damp.

When I arrived back at the dormitory, it was empty. Perhaps morning tube-clearing was a bathroom event. I certainly hoped so.

I packed up my panniers and took them outside into the sun. I wouldn't need my coat anyway, which was good because my coat was still damp. With a key from the warden, I fetched Scott from the bike shed. Scott, of course, was still damp as well.

I decided to attach my wet trainers and my wet coat on top of the panniers with bungies to give them chance to dry in the sun and used my spray can of oil on Scott's chain.

As I was doing that, Guy Three appeared.

"Nice bike."

I decided not to ask after his tubes. "Thank you," I said. "We've done a few miles together."

I patted Scott's saddle.

"Don't push it," Scott said.

"Where are you from?" I asked Guy Three.

"Aberdeen. Come up for the weekend."

He was young-ish, possibly slightly hung over, and there was something about the eyes that suggested it might be as well not to ask too many questions.

"Well," I said. "Won't stop. I'm going to look around

33

Kirkwall before I carry on."

"Aye. See you." He didn't ask where I was going in my cycling kit, which struck me as unusual.

Scott and I mooched into town, which was mostly Sunday-morning-closed, but it was a good place for mooching. The main street was narrow and stone-flagged, with stone or rendered houses and shops on either side, and the odd tree set in the pavements. The shops looked unlike most British towns – family-owned and slightly quirky. Tourists were definitely catered for, and there were tourist items to be bought, but there were also smaller traditional shops. Kirkwall might be the capital of Orkney, but it was not a big place and the major chainstores had not made inroads as yet.

The cathedral was built of large sandstone blocks in a range of colours – reds, golds and pale yellows. Up to door height there was an order to the colours – red, yellow, red, yellow – but above that the stonemasons seemed to have used any blocks that came to hand. There were patches of yellow and red, and odd blocks of one colour in amongst the other.

The high doors were locked. It was too early. I had seen photos though. Inside were imposing Norman-like pillars of red sandstone stretching up to a high vaulted roof, and a long nave leading to tall bright windows above the altar.

When it was built, the Orkney Islands were Norse. Vikings had come as raiders and traders originally, using the islands as a stopping off point for a bit of rape and pillage in Britain and Ireland, Iceland and Greenland, France and right down to the Mediterranean. But then the Norse settled here and in northern and western Scotland, many becoming farmers and fishermen, and eventually Christian.

Earl Rognvald, an excellent name I decided, was the man behind the cathedral. He dedicated it to his uncle, Earl Magnus, who had become Saint Magnus when his head came into close contact with an axe-head. Very Viking. So this was the Cathedral of St Magnus. I decided to potter down to the harbour before coming back to have a look inside.

The road narrowed and twisted as we slipped through the town towards the sea, then opened up to a broad road and the harbour opposite. Fishing boats were tied up ahead of me. Round the bay to the left was what could have been an oil terminal with big white containers and a small passenger liner. To the right at the end of a wide pier was a marina, with a mix of sailing and motor boats rocking in the stiff breeze, the sun shining on their white hulls.

I leaned Scott against a wall advertising ferries to Shetland and walked along the pier. A man was looking down at the sailing boats. His back was to me, but I seemed to recognise his shape. He sneezed loudly and turned.

"Hey," he said in an Aberdonian sort of way, and he sniffed loudly.

"Hi."

Silence.

"I'd like to have a boat," he said.

"Mm.

"A 35-footer. Better than a house."

"Oh?"

"Could just sail away."

"Right," I said.

"Some folks say I'm a loner, but I jus' like doing my own thing."

A bit longer silence.

"Well," I said. "Can't stop." Silence. "Long way to go."

"Aye. See you."

Though not if I saw him first.

I cycled back up into town and bought sandwiches for later from a busy little bakers. A café was open and I had a coffee until I thought the cathedral might be open, but when I got there, there was a sign. A service had started and it was closed to the public.

As I turned away from the cathedral, a familiar voice said, "Are you following me?"

"What? No."

He stalked off.

I walked the other way, round the side of the cathedral. There was certainly a service on; I could hear singing through the wooden side door. I was disappointed not to see inside, but was satisfied with the thought that I now had a perfect excuse to come back. I liked Kirkwall and I quite liked the idea that I would have to come back one day. There was a good chance that Guy Three wouldn't be there any more.

On the other side of the road stood the stone ruins of the Earl's Palace, tall and imposing against the grass surrounding them, aloof amongst trees swaying in the wind and sun. There were low-slung turrets and dark doorways, and I could have happily explored the ruins and the neighbouring Bishop's Palace, but it was time to go. I had had an unscheduled 46 miles yesterday, and my mind turned to that wind blowing the trees. This was meant to be a shorter day to give me time to see Kirkwall, but cycling and wind don't go together.

Besides, I didn't really want to risk bumping into Guy Three again.

"Scott," I said, pointing him in the general direction of out of town. "Southwards."

I got lost cycling out of Kirkwall.

Half way up a considerable hill, still within Kirkwall, I panted up to a lady with a pram. Fitness not being my strong point at this stage, I said something like, "Which… way… is… Burwick?"

Burwick was the harbour for my ferry later on in the day. It was not actually on Mainland at all, but causeways had been built linking four islands together during the Second World War. Burwick was on South Ronaldsay.

She set me on my way, further uphill, on the road that

would lead me past the Highland Park Distillery, Orkney's larger producer of Scotch whisky.

"Scott," I said. "I hereby vow never to knowingly pass by a distillery."

"Not knowingly pass in what sense?"

"I intend, Scott, to purchase a miniature bottle of whisky in every distillery I pass."

"One of the greater aims in life," he said.

"I thought so."

Low buildings appeared ahead of me on either side of the road, together with a roof line which I hoped to see more than once. The Highland Park Distillery had the distinctive distillery-chimney, complete with paddy-field hat on top. Wonderful.

I had done my research. The making of malt whisky, I had discovered from Michael Jackson's Malt Whisky Companion (a man of many talents that Michael Jackson), was a mix of art, science and industry. Single malts are whiskies which are distilled in just one place, with the distinctive local flavours developing from peat-smoke, seaweed or salt-laden sea-air, from the previous use of aging-barrels for sherry or bourbon, the heather of surrounding moors, the local spring water, the oak of the barrels, the shape of the stills, the…

The combinations were almost endless, and I was looking forward to my first distillery.

At Highland Park, I had read, I could expect a House-style that was '*smoky and full-flavoured*', with older vintages suited to '*a book at bedtime*'. The 15-year-old malt would have a Nose of '*soft apricot, over-ripe pear, toasted almond and beech nut*', a Palate that balanced '*caramelised fruit, honey and heathery smoke*', and a Finish of '*treacle toffee*'.

I pulled in by the buildings next to the road. The Highland Park Malt Whisky Distillery was closed on a Sunday morning.

I was disappointed, but resolute.

"Scott," I said, "I will return."

The hill continued beyond the town, and with the wind in my face, it felt tough. At the top I stopped to take in the view. Behind me was a great expanse of land and sea. First there were the roofs of Highland Park and of the town below. The cathedral stood proud off to the left. Beyond that, the liner reflected brightly against the sun, and western Mainland looped green around the large bay. On the horizon straight north lay a whisper of more Orkney islands.

But Scott was facing south now. There were grassy fields stretching away downhill to Mainland's eastern arm. The road fell away ahead of me, with bungalows and farmhouses dotting the land, though not a single tree. A bay cut into the land, circled with sand. The sea was calmer there, protected by the hills and ridges of west Mainland and the cliffs of Hoy. I was looking down at Scapa Flow. Somewhere down there, maybe the group of buildings by the water, was the Scapa Distillery. (House-style: '*Salt, hay. Oily, spicy chocolate. After a hearty walk, before dinner*'). Another one missed.

The wind was strong in my face, and the sun was bright in a sky strewn with puffs of high clouds. I leaned Scott against a wall and delved into my front pannier for sunscreen. I had been very pleased when I had bought it; it was an 'anti-aging sun defence cream'. Anti-aging. That's what I needed. I plastered it on my face. If I aged at all on this trip, I'd be taking the cream back to the shop.

I considered the wind again. My mum, I thought, would call this 'a good drying day'. I pulled my bag of damp clothes out of a pannier. It would take a bit of ingenuity to rig up a washing line on Scott, but it was surely possible. My bike lock, I thought, was a long, curly one, like one of those slinky toys that curled over themselves to walk downstairs when I was a boy. It took quite a bit of threading to work two pairs of (washed) underwear and the sleeves of a bright red bike shirt over the concertina of the lock, but I managed it, then fixed the bike lock between the saddle and the back of the pannier.

I was left holding two pairs of (washed) socks. I looked at Scott. The front pannier had a little pocket on either side. I stuck one half of each pair of socks into the pockets, leaving the other half hanging out to catch the breeze and sun.

I stood back to admire my work. With the red bike shirt and underpants at the back and socks sticking out like ears at the front, Scott did look slightly un-mountain-bike-like, but this was no time to admit that. I whistled as I re-mounted.

We set off down the long hill, underpants flapping in the wind behind me.

"Dignity," I shouted above the wind, "is overrated."

Something strange was happening as I cycled downwards. I was having to pedal very hard to move. Why is it that when you are on a bike, the wind is always in your face? I checked my bike computer. Downhill, pedalling hard, and I was going at about 12mph. It was tough going.

In fields on either side, there were odd concrete buildings. Some had no windows, and just sat there eyeless in the middle of fields. I was changing century. This was not the 21st century, or even the era of Skara Brae or the Vikings. I was back in two world wars, when Scapa Flow was turned into a large-scale port for the Royal Navy. From here the Navy combated German fleets operating from the Baltic, and the concrete blocks might have housed munitions, or ship-parts, or sailors facing enemy submarines out in the cold Atlantic.

At the end of the First World War, 74 German naval vessels were brought here while peace talks were conducted in Paris. When the German Admiral picked up the impression that the peace talks were foundering, he decided that his fleet could not be allowed to fall into British hands and he gave the order to sink his own fleet. On every German ship, the seawater was pumped in and the German seamen abandoned ship as their vessels sank to the bottom of Scapa Flow, where many remain.

However, the saddest ship on the sea-floor dates from the Second World War.

As I cycled, with Scapa Flow always on my right, I passed a sign. 'Royal Oak viewpoint'. In October 1939, a German submarine crept between the block-ships intended to prevent access to Scapa Flow by the enemy. Torpedo tubes were lined up on The Royal Oak as it lay at anchor. Two torpedoes hit the ship, and it sank fast.

833 men drowned, and still lie in the official war grave under the waters of Scapa Flow.

It was a sobering thought.

I turned a corner beyond the village of St Mary's and there was the first of the 'Barriers' that join the eastern ring of islands around Scapa Flow.

Winston Churchill came to Orkney after the tragedy of The Royal Oak, and gave orders to block access for enemy submarines to Scapa Flow by building barriers linking Mainland to the tiny Lamb Holm, from there to Glimps Holm, to Burray, and then to the island of South Ronaldsay.

Rock would be quarried on the islands and dropped into channels. Giant blocks of concrete would be added, and finally a road on top. By 1942 a lack of manpower was holding up the building. It was then that Italian prisoners of war began to be brought to the islands to help with the building. Captured in the heat of North African battle, 1,300 Italians found themselves in the Orkney Islands.

I cycled across the first causeway on the modern tarmac A-road towards the island of Lamb Holm. Huge concrete blocks lay higgledy-piggledy on either side, the sea lapping against them. At the far end of the barrier, behind a small hill, flew an Italian flag. It would mark one of the main places I had planned to visit on Orkney. The Italian Chapel.

Some of the Italians were housed in Nissen huts on Lamb Holm. They had most things they wanted, a theatre and a recreation hut, all constructed using their growing skills in the use of concrete. Even the billiard table was made from concrete.

One of the Italians, an artist called Domenico Chiocchetti, had even created a sculpture of St George and the Dragon out of concrete and barbed wire.

But they didn't have a chapel.

In 1943, the camp commander set aside two Nissen huts for them. Placed end-to-end, the semi-circular corrugated-iron huts didn't seem like a church. So over the next two years, the Italians, led by Chiocchetti, plaster-boarded the inside, concreted the outside, built a frontage, created a cast iron altar screen and a concrete altar, and – most extraordinarily – painted the inside to mimic the pillars, the carvings and the ceiling of an Italian church.

Chiocchetti had not quite finished creating the font when the war finished. So he stayed on to complete the work.

He was invited back in 1960 to restore his own paintings. A service of re-dedication was attended by 200 locals and was played on Italian radio. He visited again in 1964 to bring wooden stations of the cross as a gift for the church, but when eight other former prisoners returned in 1992, he was too ill to be among them. He died in 1999, an extraordinary man. I was looking forward to seeing his work.

Scott and I climbed the small hill and turned into the car park. At the far end stood the small white-painted frontage of the chapel. Twin white columns marked the entrance. Sloping roof lines were topped off with carvings, a cross and a small bell tower. The face of Jesus in his crown of thorns was picked out in red.

I leant Scott against a wall and peaked around the side of the chapel. True enough, the rounded roof of a Nissen hut was just behind.

"Scott," I said. "Lunch first." I was hungry. Cars came and went as I ate my sandwiches, a steady stream of visitors to the chapel. At first I was warm in the sun, sheltered from the wind, just in shorts and a cycling top. But as I finished eating, I felt a chill and the day became suddenly dark. I looked up at what had been a blue sky. It wasn't blue now. From nowhere, black clouds had blown over. I felt the first drop as I put my rubbish back in a bag. The second and third drops followed pretty quickly, and without warning, it began pelting down with rain.

My damp clothes, wet shoes and waterproof jacket were firmly bike-locked to the panniers on the back of Scott. I desperately needed shelter to sort myself out. I looked at the church door and thought of Chiocchetti's masterpieces inside. No, I couldn't take Scott inside. I wheeled him quickly round to the down-wind side of the chapel, hunching myself over the clothes on the pannier, feeling the rain soaking my back. I managed to release my jacket and shrug it on over my wet bike shirt, found my keys from my rucksack pocket and undid the bike lock, pulled a plastic bag over the saddle, then sprinted, wet clothes and shoes in my hands, inside the chapel. It was a stone floor. Actually it was probably concrete. Either way, I dropped a tangle of wet bike-shirt/underwear/shoes/rucksack on the floor, and shivered damply. A young couple were watching me, a little mesmerised.

"It's raining," I said.

They looked at each other, then back at me.

"I'm on my bike," I said. "Bit wet."

"You should have brought your bike in." She was dark-haired, young and pretty, and she was dry. I wasn't many of those things.

"Bye then," her partner said, opening the wooden door and looking at the sky. "Hope it dries up for you."

"Yes. Thanks."

I was alone now, so I abandoned the pile of clothes on the floor, and raised my eyes to the chapel walls. A carved frieze ran around the chapel low down. Above that, brickwork curved right up over my head and down to the frieze on the far side. But the frieze wasn't carved, and the brickwork was not bricks. The fancy pillars either side of the door were not pillars at all. The roof ribs were not really stone. All of them were painted on to the flat inside surfaces of the domed Nissen hut.

I walked forward to the altar screen delicately made in iron. Beyond, the walls and ceiling were even more lavish. The Virgin Mary and Baby Jesus emerged from painted sunshine and heavenly clouds. There was even a (painted) shadow of the clouds against the (painted) stonework behind.

The delicate altar table seemed carved of white stone, yet I knew it was made of concrete. On either side of the altar were twin stained-glass windows, actually part of the painting. In alcoves (not real alcoves) on either side, pairs of angels made ready their heavenly music, while on the curved ceiling above was stone tracery, a bluer sky than outside, a dove of peace, and the animals representing the Gospel-writers, Matthew, Mark, Luke and John.

I moved to the back of the church to find Chiocchetti's font, another delicate construction. It was a hexagonal bowl with the faces of angels, supported by a narrow twisted column. Actually made from concrete on a frame of barbed wire.

The Visitors Book was open on a table. I scanned the page and was astonished. There was a signature so shaky that I could not read it, but another, firmer hand had written after it, '*Helped to build the chapel 1942-45*'. Underneath, the same hand had written, '*Proud to escort NONO (above) on his first journey back in 63 years*'.

I was moved just to be reading the entry. Nono, I thought, should be very proud of being part of the building. As should the Orcadians who maintain the building.

I opened the door to look at the weather. The rain had passed over, leaving the ground soaking. With my pile of clothes from the floor, I made my way around to Scott. He was soaking as well.

A car door slammed and a moment later a voice said, "I'd have taken the bike inside, if I were you. I saw you from the car. You must have got pretty wet."

He was about my age, dark hair, friendly face, and a wife waiting patiently to go into the chapel.

"I thought about it," I said. "But I didn't like to take a bike into a church."

"I don't think anyone would have minded."

"No, I suppose so."

"Where are you going to?" he asked.

"Well, tonight as far as John O'Groats."

"And after that?"

"To the border with England eventually. I hope. Are you here on holiday?"

"We are. We'd heard about the chapel. Had to come."

"Take a look at the Visitors Book," I said. "There's quite an entry on today's page."

"I will. And take care."

The black clouds had gone as fast as they had arrived, and it seemed that the Italian Chapel had appeared at exactly the right moment. Scott might have got wet, but I was mostly dry.

I gave Scott a shake. Quite a bit of water fell off, though the bag on the saddle had worked. So at least my rear end would not be sitting on a wet sponge.

My saddle was designed for comfort. It had springs built into it, and was thickly padded with gel. One slight issue was that it absorbed rainwater all too easily and sliding up and down on a wet spongy saddle did tend to make the shorts and underwear a bit damp and unpleasant.

Another causeway on to little Glimps Holm island, and then another, dead straight, with jumbled concrete blocks either side. Off to the left lay an upside-down rusting hulk of ship. In fact, more than one. And another off to the right. I stopped at the far end of the causeway. The rusting ships must have been the block ships designed to stop German submarines before the Barriers were built. Next to the largest of the hulks were tethered what I took to be lobster or crab pots, and a couple of small fishing boats were swinging against their anchors.

I was taking photographs in a once-more sunny day, when I glanced up the road to find a young woman walking towards me. She had long dark hair blowing in the wind, and a very large rucksack on her back.

"Hi," I said. "Did you get very wet?"

"Non." Now that sounded French. "I could see eet, but eet meessed me." Definitely French.

She smiled, and it was a nice smile. She couldn't have been much more than 21 or 22, and it felt bizarre to meet this young Frenchwoman here on an island in the Orkney Islands, me heading south with my gear, her heading north with an enormous pack.

"And you?" she asked.

"No, not really. I sheltered in the Italian Chapel."

"Oh, is zat on zee next island?"

"The one after. Not too far. That's a big pack. You look like you're walking a long way?"

She undid her rucksack's belt and swung the bag expertly

on to the floor. She was evidently used to doing that.

It was quite an adventure. She had taken the ferry from her home in Brittany to Ireland, then walked up through Ireland to Belfast. From there she had taken a ferry to Glasgow and walked all the way up to Cape Wrath, the far northwest point of Scotland. She had hitched-hiked to John O'Groats, then taken the ferry to Orkney.

She perched on a boulder and I leaned on Scott. She seemed pleased to talk, and it occurred to me that maybe if you walk and camp, you don't really talk to too many people.

"That's quite a walk," I said. "So where are you going now?"

"Shetland. And Norway. And maybe 'ome."

"Amazing."

It was an astonishing trip, but I wished that she had somebody to share the experience with. She looked as though she needed someone. Shetland. Norway. Home. That was a long walk, and I wondered to myself what had set her off on the solo journey in the first place. I sensed that I shouldn't ask.

She asked after my journey and I told her my route.

"You should cycle in France," she said. "Ferry to Brittany, down to Bordeaux, across zee Dordogne and zee Auvergne."

"I'd love to."

We chatted about Orkney, the lack of trees, the wind, the beauty of the place. And it still felt bizarre.

We said goodbye and wished each other well. She held out her hand to shake mine and she said, "I em Christine."

"I'm Mike."

She hefted her pack on to her back, smiled and set off across the causeway. At the top of a little hill I looked back. She was part way across the Barrier, still going north. She was tiny against the black tarmac, with those grey blocks and rusting ships in the sea on either side, and the grassy island beyond her.

"And I'm Scott," Scott said.

"You can shut up."

The clouds might have gone, but the wind had not. If anything it was stronger, and I was fed up with it by now.

At the start of the fourth of the Barriers there were public loos in a car park and I pulled in. As I did so, four or five cars followed me. Each had a trailer with one or two kayaks on the back. Drivers and passengers jumped out, all really excitable, chattering away to each other as they started unloading the kayaks and finding paddles.

The kayaks were lean, mean beasts, tapered at each end, yet all were different, personalised by what must be the members of a club.

"Will the wind not blow you about?" I asked a young-ish man with a spring in his step.

"No. These go pretty straight."

"Fantastic place."

"It's brilliant here," he said. "If you want somewhere with great wildlife, with peace and quiet, and where you don't have to lock your front door, this is the place for you. After all, if I locked the front door, how would the postman put a parcel in the hall when I am out?"

"Well, true."

"See you. Must go. Have a good ride."

He bounced over to his kayak, hauled it up and disappeared after his friends through the high reeds and sand dunes towards the sea.

The rain started again. Dark clouds were again driving across the sky at high speed, and once more the rain was heavy. I wheeled Scott into a gap between the loos and a sand dune, reckoning on waiting it out.

I ate a chocolate bar. I didn't hurry.

"It isn't stopping," I said to Scott when we had been there for ten minutes. "And standing behind public loos can get you a reputation."

I waited another couple of minutes then decided the rain had closed in for the day.

"We'll go for it," I said.

It took another few minutes to put on my wet-weather gear in full, and then we set off across the causeway into a roaring wind blowing big drops of rain into my face. Each push down on the pedals was an effort, as the gale tried to keep me on Burray island and to stop me arriving on South Ronaldsay.

"Balderdash," I said. Or something like that.

The rain lasted about ten minutes. After which it stopped again as quickly as it had started and the sun came out. I still had the wind though, buffeting me about. I had two choices. I could keep going south all the way to the bottom of South Ronaldsay and get the ferry from Burwick. That would be about eight miles straight into the gale. At the ridiculously slow speed I was going, that would probably take an hour or so, and every now and then I would feel as though a bucket of water had been thrown over my head.

Or I could cut off right to the village of St Margaret's Hope and get a different ferry. That was about two miles.

St Margaret's Hope was marked on the map with a little symbol of a full beer glass. No matter how hard I looked at the map, Burwick didn't have that little symbol.

St Margaret's Hope was indeed a nice little place, its few houses grouped around the harbour and slipway. The houses were impressive – solid stone constructions with stepped roof lines and small windows. Built to keep out northerly storms perhaps.

The ferry port was around the bay to the west, a little like the arrangement at Thurso. I cycled there and found a small ticket office. The next ferry was a couple of hours off, and so I headed back into the village and found a wall to lean Scott against.

The sun was out and I unpacked my wet washing again and draped the two pairs of underpants, red bike shirt and trainers completely across Scott.

"Sorry about this."

"No, you're not."

"No. I suppose I'm not really. I'm going to find the pub."

Actually, it wasn't a full glass of beer that I was after. What I most wanted was a nice cup of tea.

There was chatter from half a dozen men around the pub's small bar, but the chatter stopped the moment I entered. It was possible that they didn't have many strangers appear wearing shorts and a bright blue bike shirt.

"Make way for the man," one said smiling. "Make way."

"Service!" another shouted through the empty bar. "There's a thirsty man here."

Space was made for me to reach the bar, and the barman appeared.

"Um, any chance of a cup of tea?"

I half expected some jokes at my expenses from the men with their pint glasses, but they were all tolerant enough of this strange cyclist in their midst. I'd be a good talking point later though.

"Cup of tea for the man," my first friend said to the barman.

I decided not to ask for lemon drizzle cake.

It was only busy around the bar and I sat at a table by the window with my pot of tea and my guide book. St Margaret's Hope was named after a St Margaret a thousand years ago, but was also the place where two hundred years later the grand-daughter of a Scots King had died on her way from Norway to England. She had been heir to the Scottish throne and betrothed to an English prince. She was a Margaret, the 'Maid of Norway' and just three years old.

Her death led to English kings' claims to Scotland, invasion, occupation and a spirit of Scotland that had never really existed before. It was a strange tangle to grow out of the death of a three-year-old girl named Margaret in the village of St Margaret's Hope in the Orkney Islands.

The sun was shining warmly as I returned to Scott, and my damp clothes were steaming nicely.

"You are multi-tasking," I said.

"Never tell."

"Of course not," I said. "Your secret is safe". I took a photograph. "Mostly."

The rain started again as we made our way along to the Portakabin that served as a waiting room for the ferry. There was nobody else there, so I wheeled Scott inside. Outside, the rain came down hard, and I was glad not to be cycling down to the southern tip of Orkney. This had been enough.

The ferry was busy, with most of the seats taken in the lounge, but I found myself a corner and stretched out in an armchair. I was warm and dry, and I could have slept for longer if I hadn't woken myself up snoring. I checked for dribble. I think I was alright.

We docked at Gills Bay, which was not much more than a pier sheltered by cliffs from the worst of the westerly storms. The cars were let off first, then Scott and I bumped up the ramp and out into a grey, drizzly late afternoon. A steep-ish hill led up out of the bay. Tired legs eased the pedals around at a stately rate, though my heart rate was probably not so stately. I stopped half way to check the map.

A couple of miles cycling found me outside John O'Groats Youth Hostel. Actually, it was more like a farmhouse than a hostel. It was off-white, two-storied, with its window-surrounds painted a dark red. It didn't really look like a hostel. And it was about three miles away from John O'Groats. So I would have had serious doubts about it being John O'Groats Youth Hostel, except that there was a sign, and the sign said it was.

"Scott, we are at John O'Groats Youth Hostel."

"Good," he said. "Can we go home now?"

The friendly lady warden signed me in with a smile. "You're in Room 6, just by the door here."

"Fine. Are there others in there or just me?"

"Oh, there's one or two more. And there's a shed for your bike."

I wheeled Scott around to the shed, removing panniers and noting a smell from somewhere.

I said, "I think my Day One trainers might stay with you tonight."

"Thank you."

"You're welcome."

I carried my panniers through into a dormitory which held three sets of double bunks and a single bed. All were taken bar two.

As I sorted out wet and dry clothing, my room-mates came in and out. They made an interesting bunch. I was sharing with a cyclist using his car to move him on to different hostels from where he would do day rides, two separate motorcyclists, one of whom had made the journey from Land's End, a silent man with his head buried in a laptop, and a young German on a touring holiday. All of them chatted amiably – except laptop-man.

I moved into the dining room to eat the sandwiches I had bought in Kirkwall, and chatted with two cyclists who had finished their ride from Land's End to John O'Groats (LEJOG, as it is known). Both were mid-twenties, wiry, windswept and bearded. They had averaged 85 miles a day over thirteen days. The warden brought through LEJOG certificates for them, and they grinned at each other, their mission accomplished, and disappeared for showers.

"Impressive," I said to John, one of my motorcycling room-mates at a table close by. He was around sixty, short, grey-bearded and almost bald. Behind his glasses, his eyes were thoughtful.

"Very," he said.

"And you?" I asked. "What brings you here on a motorbike?"

"Ah. I had a friend who was terminally ill. We were in a motorbike club together. He left me his motorbike in his will. It's a 1963 Triumph. Well, anyway, my wife died as well, and I thought, well, I would ride from Land's End to John

O'Groats in their memory."

Perhaps I understood the thoughtful look in his eyes.

"I always carry some photos with me," John said. "Would you like to see them?"

"Yes, of course."

He took half a dozen photos from his wallet and passed the first to me. It was of a silvery-blue and chrome motorbike, with it's small black number-plate running the length of the mudguard over the front wheel.

"This was my friend's bike. The 1963 Triumph," he said, and he told me how he had come to meet his friend at the club and some of their adventures.

The second photo was of a different motor bike. As was the third, fourth, fifth and sixth. For each photo he had a small story of his wife or his friend, though neither of them appeared in any of the photos. Each time he told a story, his eyes took him further away.

"Thank you, John," I said, when he had told me all his tales. "Those photos are wonderful."

I passed him back his precious pictures.

He said, "I'll set off home tomorrow. Just hoping the Triumph gets me there."

"I'm sure it will. Safe journey to you. Take care, won't you?"

Captain's log: Day Two

Target:	22.0 miles	35.2 Km
Actual distance:	19.9 miles	31.8 Km
Average speed:	9.5 mph	15.2 Kmph
Maximum speed:	25.5 mph	40.8 Kmph
Total distance:	66.0 miles	105.6 Km

I was thoughtful as I got into bed. The dreaded YHA sheet sleeping bag felt such a minor inconvenience. Tomorrow I would set off from John O'Groats on my own journey south. I had a long way to go as well.

Day Three

Target: 35 miles / 56 Km
The north coast from John O'Groats to Dounreay
via The Castle of Mey and Thurso

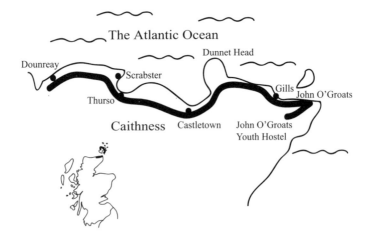

The bike-shed door creaked as I opened it.

"How was your night?" I said.

"I could have done without the trainers."

"I was talking to the trainers."

We eased off down the lane towards the ocean. It was three miles downhill to John O'Groats. There was pale blue sky and wispy cloud above, while ahead of us in a dark blue sea lurked the little green island of Stroma. Behind it lay the fainter outlines of the Orkney Islands. It was fabulous.

John O'Groats seemed to consist of new-looking craft shops and a low, white-painted and much older 'Last House' with stone flags for a roof and a small turret entrance. The Last House, a gift shop now of course, looked down on the little harbour below. There were no fishing boats today, but lobster pots were stacked against a wall, and I hoped that the piers had a practical use, as well as giving room to another gift shop selling postcards and tartan hats.

The car park was being swept, and the shops were starting to open, but nobody had yet brought out the famous John O'Groats signpost with its legend of '874 miles to Land's End'. It belongs to a local business which charges for photographs, and the photographer was perhaps having a lie-in, so there was no queue of walkers or cyclists or pushers-of-bathtubs all the way from Land's End.

I tried not to look too hard at the fenced-off, empty and run-down John O'Groats Hotel, with its pointy towers and big windows. It would have been the perfect place to find the John O'Groats Youth Hostel, but instead it was derelict, and that was a sad sight. On such a beautiful day though, I would ignore it.

I leant Scott against a fence post guarding the well-trimmed grass bank that fell away towards the sea, balanced the camera on a bench and set the timer. Surprisingly, it worked, and I have a photo of a resplendent bike, a blue-coated cyclist with a smile, and in the background the Last House and the ocean.

I pushed Scott down to the harbour where I found a signpost painted on the wall of the pier. This signpost, I noticed, reckoned that Land's End was 876 miles away, with London 690 miles, the North Pole 2200 miles and Orkney just 6 miles. I felt a bit of a fraud. I may have cycled round Orkney to reach John O'Groats, but I couldn't really compete with most of the cyclists arriving here.

A voice came from up the slope.

"I thought it was you."

John was walking down to join me, his 1963 Triumph back up in the car park.

"John!" I said, pleased to meet up again. He was such a genuine, quiet man. "Good to see you. Would you like me to take a photo of you with the signpost?"

"Well, yes please. And I could take a photo of you."

I took a photograph of him on his camera and he took one of me on mine; he at the end of a journey, me really only starting. We shook hands, wished each other well, and I waved him off. It only occurred to me later that the photos he showed of his journey would not feature himself at all. Just the trusty 1963 Triumph.

The plan was to cycle westwards along the north coast of Scotland for two days, before cutting down through

Sutherland towards Inverness. For the moment, though, I was in Clan Sinclair country. Here in Caithness and in Orkney, the Sinclairs had dominated for centuries. My grandmother had been a Sinclair, although admittedly from a branch of the Scottish clan in England. In fact, on the other side of London. It would certainly be interesting to know how and why the Sinclair family found themselves in Kent. Perhaps when I got home, I should investigate. I could always come back and lay claim to my vast family estates later.

Cycling westwards, the wind was inevitably from the west, but it wasn't strong and the cycling was gorgeous. It was the main road, but with very little traffic and the sea always close by. After a few miles I had a choice of Sustrans Cycle Route One taking me on country lanes inland and over hills, or the A-road continuing to hug the coast.

"Scott, we are going to use the A-road."

"That's not like you."

"These are A-roads, Scottie, but not as we know them."

"Don't call me Scottie."

"Sorry."

Like mainland Orkney, this stretch of mainland Scotland was undulating with a distinct lack of trees. So when I started to get glimpses of some turrets surrounded by a small wood, I knew I must be approaching the Castle of Mey, the Scottish home of the Queen Mother when she was alive.

We turned off down a long drive into the woods, and this led round to the seaward side of the castle and possibly one of the most picturesque car parks in the country, with its view down a sloping lawn to the ocean and across to Orkney. I had wondered why the Queen Mother might have chosen to spend a month or two of her year here every year. This view seemed to be part of the answer.

I leaned Scott against the wall of a new tea-shop cum gift-shop, and took full advantage of the tea-shop. They were offering 'Queen Mother's Cake', containing dates and walnuts, which probably had lots of vitamins. And protein.

Definitely fibre.

It might just fend off the scurvy.

The walled garden was surprisingly plain, but then perhaps the gardeners had over the years planted flowers which bloomed in the seasons when the Queen Mother would have been in residence.

A door in the garden's high wall led to the lawn behind the castle itself. On the far side was a 5-storey-high tower which might have been the original castle built by the Sinclairs. That had been added to several times over the centuries, and every corner had a little turret in traditional Scottish-castle style. I counted nine turrets just on the side of the castle I could see, and the building was not that big.

The front door of the castle led into a two-storey hallway, with twin curving staircases leading up to a balcony and the main rooms. A pale blue coat hung on the coat-stand by the door.

"The coat," said the lady in her Castle of Mey uniform, "was the Queen Mother's coat. She liked blue."

"Did you know her then?"

"Yes, of course. My family have been farm managers here for years. When my husband died, she appointed my sons instead, even though they were only twenty-one."

The Queen Mother had first seen the empty castle in 1952 when visiting a friend further along the coast. She had bought and restored it, and then spent every August and October here until she died at the age of 101. Even at that age and walking with a stick, she would resist any attempt to help her up the staircases.

"She must have loved the place," I said, "to keep coming back."

"Oh, I think so."

I toured each room, chatting to the talkative ladies minding their former mistress's house. In the dining room, laid out for a feast with crystal and silver, I learned that the Queen Mother would only drink water and champagne with a meal, and afterwards would switch to Martini and lemonade, stirred, not shaken.

So far, the accents of the room-guides had been local, but this one was not, and I asked where she was from.

"We moved up from Lancashire when inheritance tax took our farm."

"That must have been hard."

"It was. We moved into a croft that had been empty for forty years. There was no electricity or water. That first winter we had fifty-mile-an-hour winds off the sea and had to hold the windows in place to stop them blowing in."

"But you stayed."

"Oh yes, it's wonderful here if you can put up with the wind."

In the lounge there were magazines on the table, photos of the Queen Mother's family, paintings by Charles and Philip, a part-drunk bottle of Martini, and high windows looking out to Orkney.

Parties there could become rowdy, and the Queen Mother had a sense of mischief. "When the equerries went on holiday," the guide said to me, "it became a tradition for them to bring her a silly present. The housekeeper at the time used to hate the things they brought back and would get rid of them. At one party here, the guests were slightly the worse for wear, and made a human pyramid to put a little stuffed tartan Nessie up out of the house keeper's reach."

She pointed high up to the top of the curtains, and there sat, well out of reach, a little stuffed tartan Nessie. I guessed it now had a permanent home there.

The room-guide told the history of the castle, and when the Sinclairs were mentioned, I told them of my Sinclair ancestry.

"Perhaps I am the true heir to the castle?" I said.

"You might just have a little trouble proving that."

My tour took me past the (unheated) bedrooms. Central heating was apparently considered unnecessary, when you could have storage heaters and hot water bottles.

"Margaret hated it here. I think she only ever stayed the night once and was so cold, she never stayed again."

Then down through the kitchens below the dining room. "It could be very noisy in here when there was a party going upstairs."

"I can imagine. Do the family still come?"

"Prince Charles does. He likes it here."

And outside in a cool sunshine, I thought, 'so do I'.

We pedalled off along the lane back towards the main road. To my right was Dunnet Head, which is the real most northerly point of mainland Britain, John O'Groats being a bit of an impostor. We headed on west, past the sand dunes around the wide spread of Dunnet Bay. At the far end, I stopped to look back. A wide and long beach, pockmarked with flat slabs of stone, shelved gently into the sea from the dunes. At the far end of the bay, the land rose into the 300-foot high cliffs that made up Dunnet Head. It was said that, even at that height, the windows of the lighthouse had been damaged by stones thrown up from the sea during the worst of the northerly storms.

Round the corner a sign appeared for Castletown and its 'Flagstone Trail'. We followed the route down to a harbour and to boards telling the story of Castletown and the time when huge quarries here produced the best flagstones in the world. Paris, London and dozens of other cities and towns were paved with stone from here. Thousands of men and women worked in the quarries, factories and harbour, chopping out the stone, trimming it to size, and shipping it by sea to pave the world. Today the area was pretty desolate, with collapsing mill buildings fenced off and weeds growing like a jungle where before there had been the most active of industry. It had all been killed off by concrete.

I sat to have a drink amidst high buttercups and grasses blowing in the breeze. Across from me was a dry-stone-wall made of flagstones and on the other side of the lane were harbour walls made of the same stone. Small boats with lobster pots were tied up in the quiet of the harbour. It was a sad place. Perhaps this had been where my Sinclair ancestors had worked. Perhaps when the jobs were gone, a great-great-grandfather of mine had gone south in search of work. It was a little more likely than my laying claim to the Castle of Mey.

We pedalled on round the coast and here there was another role for the flagstones. Up-ended, they became low walls to gardens or fields, set like tall, thin teeth into the ground, with a slight overlap to prevent sheep from finding a way through.

A straight and mostly flat A-road with very little traffic took me into Thurso. The town centre had its back to the beach and the sea, with four-square sandstone buildings and newer little shopping precincts. It felt busy after my travels so far, but didn't have a feeling of prosperity. It seemed likely to have a bike shop though, and my enquiries sent me to one in a little row of shops.

The bike shop was a packed place, long and narrow, with bike bits hanging everywhere. I had no idea what most of them were for. Another problem I always had in bike shops was answering simple questions.

Like what sort of spare inner tube I wanted.

"What sort of inner tube are you looking for?"

I may have looked a little vague.

Fortunately the lady had a tolerant smile, and she cast the quickest of glances out the door at Scott.

"That's fine," she said. "One spare inner tube."

"Thank you. Oh, and do you have any cable ties?"

"Cable ties?"

"Yes."

She looked at me dubiously.

"For emergencies," I said.

She reached under the counter, and emerged with a handful of little black plastic cable ties.

"How much are they?" I asked.

"Oh, I won't charge you for those. Let's hope you don't need them."

A bakery in town had a small café and I ordered a sandwich and a coffee. A black coffee was set on the counter by a uniformed waitress.

"Shall I shove some milk in that?" she asked.

'Shove'. I think perhaps she had trained as a game-keeper.

Afterwards I crossed the road to the war memorial. There were certainly Sinclairs, though they were outnumbered by Swansons and Mackays, so perhaps Thurso was on the edge of Clan Sinclair land. Perhaps I couldn't stake a claim to Thurso.

I had been surprised to read that the Scottish clans were not all Celtic by origin. I had just sort of assumed that they were. In fact, the name Sinclair came from the French lords who invaded England with William the Conqueror. The 'St Clair' family were invited into Scotland by a Scots King and had been given or married into land as far afield as Caithness and Orkney, and Roslin, south of Edinburgh. Not all those called Sinclair today have a French-Norman past; most must be a good mix of Norse and Picts, with the odd Irish-Scottish and Flemish blood mixed in. Other clans would have blood lines in different mixtures, some more Norse, some more Celtic.

The clans developed as extended families from around the year 1000AD onwards. Each had a chief who was responsible for protecting the clan and upholding their honour. As a result of which, each clan usually had quite a lot of hereditary enemies. MacDonalds and Campbells raided and murdered each other for centuries. Apparently Sinclairs weren't that keen on Campbells either, though I hadn't noticed any hereditary animosity in myself as yet. I would watch out for it.

I picked the A-road rather than the cycle route again as we carried on westwards. I wanted to see Dounreay, the nuclear plant, or, I should say, the former nuclear plant.

Dounreay was closing down, but it was a mighty long closure programme. It had last produced electricity in 1994, but would be decades before decommissioning was finished. In fact, Dounreay was still taking on apprentices, and those apprentices might reach retirement before the plant was finally closed.

I could see Dounreay from some way off, its golf-ball buildings and 5-storey office blocks visible amidst the rolling greenery. It was a big site. It would have been a vital employer for the area in its day, and there must surely be mixed feelings about it closing. There was the loss of jobs, but also the reports of radioactive particles found on the local beaches.

The buildings loomed larger as I got closer and then, as I began cycling past them at a short distance, a road led away to the right towards the nuclear site.

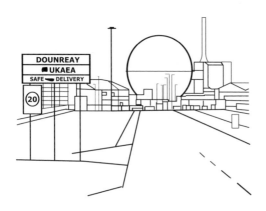

I stopped to look, and a herd of skittish young bullocks ran up to me, eyes watching me from behind a sign:

VULCAN NAVAL REACTOR
TEST ESTABLISHMENT

Vulcans? Well, it seemed a little unlikely, but you could never tell.

The nuclear plant was so out of place here, but then flagstone field-walls were a reminder that other industries have come and gone, as have many of the clanspeople of the area. I cycled on past cattle and sheep in lush pastures, past marshy ground with little cotton-wool-topped plants, and past flagstone-roofed farmhouses. In the distance were dark hills and mountains, and they did not bode at all well for my journey tomorrow.

The guest house was a low white building, with rooms to let in the roof. My hosts gave me a tour of the garden, which merged peacefully into open farmland, the only discordant note coming from the electricity pylons which drove their way across the landscape southwards.

"Do you know what they're doing?" the lady of the house said, a belligerent tone in her voice.

They?

"Um, no."

"Replacing them with even bigger ones. And do you know why?"

"Er, no."

"To supply electricity to the English."

"Oh."

"And don't get me started on that one."

I decided that was wise.

Captain's log: Day Three

Target:	35.0 miles	56.0 Km
Actual distance:	38.4 miles	61.5 Km
Average speed:	11.5 mph	18.4 Kmph
Maximum speed:	27.0 mph	43.2 Kmph
Total distance:	104.4 miles	167.1 Km

Washed and brushed, I came down for the evening meal I had booked.

"Where are you heading for?" my host asked.

"The border."

She looked at me, and I thought, 'Don't get her started on that one.'

"That," I said, "looks delicious."

Day Four

Target: 33 miles / 53 Km
The north coast from Dounreay to Tongue
via Strathy and Bettyhill

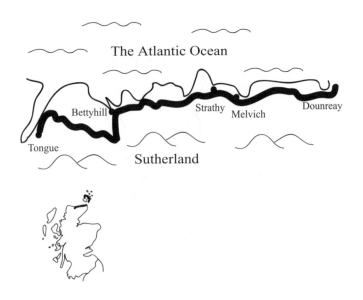

With my map propped up against salt and pepper pots, I counted the little black arrows showing 'Steep Hills' on today's route. Five steep up, seven steep down, which felt a bit odd and just slightly alarming. I couldn't believe how much the route wiggled and twitched across the map as the land rose and fell. I would be starting at sea level and finishing at sea level, heading east to west, but half the time the road seemed to be switch-backing northwards or southwards.

There was good news though. At exactly one third of the way and two thirds of the way, the map had that familiar little symbol of a full beer glass. Surely there would be a pub sign outside each of them showing a frothing glass of amber liquid and the welcoming name of the pub in a scroll underneath: 'The Full Beer Glass'. I decided that today was going to be a Formula One-style '2-stop strategy', only a bit slower.

I moved the map away from my plate of bacon and eggs, and contemplated the window. Overnight it had rained hard. It looked like the rain had stopped, though there was a still strong wind blowing out there.

"Where are you heading for tonight?"

"Westwards. As far as Tongue."

"Not too far then."

"Mm."

"Hilly though."

"Mm."

I retrieved Scott from his spot next to the washing machine in the shed and we set off, the road dipping and then climbing for the first long hill of the day. The wind gusted up from the south against my left shoulder. I had to concentrate hard to keep in a roughly straight line. The legs weren't too keen on this.

Around me, the land changed from cattle and sheep fields to rougher higher pasture and bogs. Grey cloud blew violently over and headed out to the oceans.

As the road rose, it swivelled into the wind and I stood up to put all my weight on to the pedals to turn them and keep moving upwards. Then the road turned northwards, and the wind picked me up and blew me up the hill.

"Scott," I said. "According to that map, this road is not a 'Steep Hill'."

"Good."

After a hard couple of miles the road finally started to fall and we dropped down to sea level, only for the road to rise sharply again.

"And nor is this."

It felt punishing. So when we came to an enclosed bus shelter a few miles short of Stop One (The Full Beer Glass of Strathy), I lurched off the saddle and pulled Scott inside. Instantly, the wind was gone. It was quiet, and I could look through the clear plastic sides of the new bus shelter and see what I had been unable to concentrate on as I rode. Mile upon mile of peaty bog. No trees, no buildings, but dark browns and dark greens, tufted and mossy, rolling away southwards, as the dark clouds rolled northwards. This was the Flow Country, home to dippers and dunlins, greenshanks and golden plovers. Today though, they were keeping their heads down. In fact, the wildlife seemed to have disappeared. The only things moving were the little cottony heads of the marsh-plants pulled off by the wind and skittering across the road.

I put an extra layer on under my coat, and ate a couple of chocolate bars

"Don't worry, Scott," I said. "We will soon be at The Full Beer Glass. I'm not sure about a beer at this time of day, but it's probably almost legendary for its cappuccinos and lemon drizzle cake."

That cheered one of us up anyway.

The village of Strathy was down in the valley, virtually at sea level again, but the map showed The Full Beer Glass up the far side of the valley. Twin black arrows on the map signified the first Steep Hill of the day. We climbed manfully, and I was fortified by the knowledge that soon we could stop, rest and be refreshed.

We rolled into the little car park. A couple came out the front door, their voices German.

"Hi. Are they open?"

"Yess, I think sso."

"For coffees and so on?"

"Yess, and the food is wery good."

"Thanks."

I leaned Scott against a wall. "I may be gone some time," I said.

Strangely, the door handle didn't seem to turn. I pulled it a couple of times, and then the door was opened from the inside.

"Yes?"

"Hello," I said brightly, though the face eying me up was lacking the degree of sympathy I was hoping for. "Are you doing coffees?"

"No."

"Oh. Or tea?"

"Closed till tonight."

"A hot chocolate maybe, only you see I - " The door had closed. I raised my voice slightly, alarm growing. "Or perhaps a slice of lemon drizzle cake?"

The door reopened.

"I could sell you a can of cold drink."

I must have shaken my head, I suppose, because the door was closed all over again.

The young German couple looked sadly at me. "No?"

"No."

I sat on a hard bench against the wall of that well-known hostelry 'The Empty Beer Glass, Not That I'm Bitter Or Anything', drank some cold water from a bottle, and watched as the couple put their bags in the car. They waved as they drove off.

I zipped my jacket up to my neck to try to keep out the wind and pulled the map out. The 2-stop strategy was in tatters. The only other stop all day was in Bettyhill, two thirds of the day's entire distance. I had been contemplating cycling out to Strathy Point, allegedly beautiful, but that would make this stretch even further. Also, the Steep Hill arrows on the map looked as though they were about to gang up on me.

There was no point sitting on the bench in the wind any longer; I was getting cold.

Big hills down and then up again took us higher and now there were rocky outcrops surrounded by heather, thistles and tufted grasses. It was good country, though it would have taken some sunshine and warmth to appreciate it properly.

Every now and again, the road dipped into a cutting and the wind eased. I decided to stop at some of these quieter points. Actually, my legs decided to stop at some of these quieter points. My brain didn't have much of a say in it.

In the distance there were real mountains. Grey hump-backed silhouettes on the horizon, both threatening and beckoning at the same time. I pulled in at a picnic stop, though picnickers were not too obvious, and leaned Scott against a table while I examined the information board. The mountains ahead were Ben Loyal and Ben Hope. Tomorrow I would be cycling between them.

Finally... finally, the road dropped long and steeply downwards into Bettyhill. Coming out of a small gorge, there was a sign for Elizabeth's Café, the Tourist Information Centre and a Museum. Excellent. The bike computer said twenty miles, but I was done in.

We swung round into the car park, where Elizabeth's Café turned out to be a stone-built, white-washed building with a slate roof and with, more importantly, customers going in and out, and waitresses with smiles. I drank three cups of tea straight down, then a pasty and chips, and started to feel normal again.

"Are you on your way to John O'Groats?" the lady in charge asked, and I wondered if she was Elizabeth.

"I've come from there," I said. "I'm heading south. Do you get many coming through on their way there?"

"Yes, quite often. Mostly cyclists where they have taken the Western Isles route. There are very few walkers these days though. There used to be more, but I can only remember one this year."

Outside, I followed a path through the graveyard to the former church which housed Strathnaver Museum, a museum of the Clearances, still a raw wound two hundred years after the events took place.

At the end of the eighteenth century, the country I had cycled through was heavily peopled, its crofters scratching a living off the poor land. For the landowner, the financial returns were tiny. Right here on this north coast, a solution was found. The people would be 'cleared' and sheep brought in instead.

The Duke of Sutherland seems to have been one of the more enthusiastic of the 'land improvers'. He owned 1.5 million acres of land, a vast estate. 1814 became known as The Year of the Burnings, as crofts were burned down and grassland destroyed. First-hand accounts are harrowing: "I was an eye witness of the scene — strong parties commenced setting fire to the dwellings till about 300 houses were in flames, the people striving to remove the sick, the helpless, before the fire should reach them. The cries of women and children — the roaring of cattle — the barking of dogs — the smoke of the fire — the soldiers — it required to be seen to be believed!"

The Duchess Elizabeth arranged for land to be made available on the coast for the crofters, but it was too little and too poor. The land still remembers though – it was named after her – 'Bettyhill', where I was now.

Throughout the highlands of Scotland, the pattern was

repeated, sometimes by absentee landowners in southern Scotland and England, sometimes by clan leaders whose fathers or grandfathers would have turned in their graves at what was done to their people.

Thousands starved and died or escaped to Glasgow and Edinburgh, into England, and of course over the seas to the United States, Canada and Australia. Upstairs in the museum, the displays all related to Clan Mackay, proudly showing mementos from around the world.

Perhaps a Sinclair had been caught up in the Clearances. Perhaps my great-great-great grandparents had been burned out of a home just like the replica croft inside the Museum, and had tramped their way south to escape, finishing up in Kent.

I made my way back to the café. Three bearded motor-bikers were filling cups from flasks. They weren't young, and had enormous bikes with powerful engines that would deal extremely well with any mid-life crisis.

"Have you come far?" I asked.

"Up through the Western Isles. We thought we'd stay at Thurso tonight. Have you been there?"

"I have."

"And what's it like? We've heard it's better than John O'Groats."

"It's different," I said. "There's definitely more hair-dressers and gamekeepers."

Elizabeth's Café was on the edge of Bettyhill. The rest of the small town was spread thinly along the coast, with fields and open ground separating homes on the hillside, and overlooking rocky inlets and sand-duned beaches. A long slow hill took me up to the centre of life – a shop, a school, even a swimming pool. I bought supplies in the shop and admired the fabulous view of the Naver estuary below, grassy slopes leading down to the blue water, with a long spit of sand beyond.

It was quiet, barely a car to be seen, the only sound that

of the wind funnelling down the valley. I liked Bettyhill. I suspected my young hairdresser friend from Thurso wouldn't. What would you do if you were a teenager living on this northern coast? It was beautiful and stark and quiet. Heaven for some. Considerably less than that for others.

The road dropped down and crossed the river, following the wide valley southwards. For the first time on my journey, there were proper trees growing in the shelter of the high valley sides. There were new houses being built, but also the ruins of crofts in fields. I wondered if there were ghosts.

Suddenly the road turned sharply westwards to climb the side of the valley. It was long and steep, the longest and steepest so far. I climbed as much as I could, and then stopped for a breather in a wind-free spot, climbing again when I had my breath back. A motorbiker roared past, thumb up to me. The road flattened, and then I was freewheeling, right the way back down into the next valley.

A sign pointed off to the right: Borgie Lodge Hotel. Well, it had been a 2-stop strategy.

When the hotel came into sight, I was uncertain at first. White-washed like most of the buildings around here, it looked very empty. I poked my nose inside experimentally and my nose told me that there was a log fire burning. My eyes told me that the entire place was carpeted in a navy, red, green and white tartan, and that there were antlers on walls, polished wood staircases, and comfy armchairs. It was everything I wanted right there and then. Well, it would be if –

"Hi. Can I help?"

A young man had appeared magically from the kitchens.

"Can I get a tea?" I asked.

"Of course. Come through to the lounge."

What a lounge it was. A massive stone fire place, huge comfortable-looking settees and armchairs, bookshelves with arrays of classic works, copies of The Shooting Times and angling magazines on coffee tables, prints of hunting scenes on the walls, and the magnificent tartan carpet all the way through. I was conscious that my windswept cycling gear didn't fit very well with the surroundings, but my host seemed not to notice.

"I've some freshly made shortbread," he said.

"Wonderful. Thank you."

I settled myself in by the log fire and took in the heat. I picked up one of the magazines. I had never realised that there were so many things that you could put on the end of a fishing line to tempt a fish.

My host reappeared with a delicate teapot, a spare pot of hot water, a china tea cup and saucer, a sugar bowl, a jug of milk, and a plate of three shortbread biscuits.

I wanted very, very much to stay.

"Is it mostly angling and shooting people you have here?"

"Mostly angling," he said, "but we do have families as well. Couple of families in now, in fact."

"And the shooting? Is it grouse?"

"No. Woodcock round here. But it's very seasonal. So's the fishing of course."

"You're not from here?" I asked.

"No, we're from Shropshire. My mother and I run the place."

"Do you miss things?"

"Not really. It's forty minutes to Thurso and Tescos."

"Not on a bike."

"And for clothes shopping, it's a couple of hours to Inverness." He smiled. "But not on a bike."

A combination of tea, shortbread biscuits and less wind saw me get up the next hill much easier than the last. The land was growing kinder as well, with cattle and sheep sharing the landscape. Small lochs had an occasional boat moored, no doubt for the fishing. It was a single-track road and I stopped now and again to let cars past. A good proportion, I noticed, had German number plates.

There were more downs and ups before I reached the long inlet from the sea called the Kyle of Tongue with breathtaking views down to sandy beaches, the last ones I would see on this northern coast.

The road turned south into the village of Tongue, which had a couple of hotels and a shop with a café. I bought supplies in the shop then found that the road to the Youth Hostel dropped sharply down towards the sea. The road was heading for a bridge, but a large house was looming on the right, set by itself with views of the sea and hills. I was very pleased to find that it was the Youth Hostel.

"Tongue Youth Hostel has been done up," I'd been told twice on my journey so far. The first person had added, "it's lost its friendliness, it's lost its soul." The second person had added, "it's really friendly now, and the warden makes home-made cakes for the guests."

The warden was a young-ish woman with a broad smile and what I took to be a slight Dutch accent. She and her partner were wardens here for the summer, and she loved the area. We chatted about my route, and then she gave me a key to a dormitory and told me I was sharing with just one other guy. She added that there were homemade cakes on a table in the hallway. I was going to like it here.

The hostel really had been done up. Everything was new and clean – the kitchen, the dining room, the lounge and the dormitories. This was what hostels should be like in the 21st century. Shame about the sheet sleeping bags, but you can't have everything.

I walked Scott around to the bike shed, and then did a little tour of the garden. Northwards, set in the sea channel lay the grassy and sandy Rabbit Islands. It was somewhere there that Bonnie Prince Charlie had lost the French gold sent to help him become King. On the other side of the channel, high on a promontory, stood the ruins of a castle – Castle Varrich, the medieval home of the chiefs of the Mackays.

Back inside I found another cyclist checking in. Anne was in her early twenties, slim and very fit-looking. She was cycling the reverse of my route through this northern part of Scotland. Only much faster.

As I heated up and then ate some soup, I chatted with an elderly English couple on a motoring tour, a German family with two young girls, and an Indian engineer – Sujir – on a two month break from his job in Los Angeles. This openness and friendliness with strangers was a big reason why I was opting to stay in hostels where possible, rather than in bed-and-breakfasts or hotels.

I sat with Sujir and Anne for a while. They had agreed to meet for breakfast at one of the hotels in Tongue in the morning, before going their separate ways. "Would you like to join us?" Anne asked me.

I considered the alternative of a couple of muesli bars and a banana. "That would be great," I said.

I was reading in my bunk when Tigger One and Tigger Two bounced in to the dormitory.

"Hi," Tigger One said. "Sorry. You asleep?"

"No, no. Just got into bed."

Tigger One had an Irish accent. "Are you the cyclist?"

"Um, yes."

"That's great. Great."

"Mm."

"And you're really cycling from one end of Scotland to the other?"

The warden must have told them my plan.

"Well, yes."

"Great. Great."

"And you?"

"Oh, me and Carlos, we're driving. He's Brazilian. We work on the cycle-taxis in Dublin city centre."

"Wow."

"It's a great way to chat up the women. I'm Danny, by the way."

Carlos hadn't said much at this point.

"So," he, Danny, Tigger One, said, "how old are you?"

"49."

"God, you don't look 49."

"Do I look older or younger?"

"No, no, you really don't look 49."

"How old are you?"

"28. God, if I could do what you're doing when I'm 49."

"49's really not that -"

"Carlos, he's 49."

I seemed to have been categorised in the 49 – 89 age group, whereas I'd have been considerably happier in the 28 – 49 age group.

Danny, I gathered, was teaching Carlos to play rugby and to speak English. Carlos was teaching Danny a wholly different way of playing football and of picking up female fares in his cycle cab without speaking English. I tried and failed to teach them how to use a sheet sleeping bag; they were giggling too much.

Danny and Carlos had taken a week off work and were driving long distances, all the time marvelling at some new experience. In Tongue they had met with two new experiences, sheet sleeping bags and a 49-year-old who could still turn the pedals of a bike.

Captain's log: Day Four

Target:	33.0 miles	52.8 Km
Actual distance:	36.7 miles	58.7 Km
Average speed:	9.2 mph	14.7 Kmph
Maximum speed:	31.0 mph	49.6 Kmph
Total distance:	141.1 miles	225.8 Km

"God. 49. You don't look 49."

"Night, Danny. Night Carlos."

"49. If I could do that…"

"Night, Danny."

Day Five

Target: 45 miles / 72 Km
From Tongue to Carbisdale Castle
via Altnaharra and Lairg

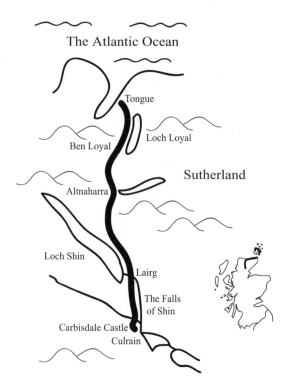

Movement and whispering in the dormitory woke me. It was still dark and I reached for my watch. Some time before five o'clock. I rolled over. A door opened and closed. The room went quiet and I went back to sleep.

I woke again to find the room awash with daylight, and empty of Danny, Carlos and their bags. I got dressed and wandered in search of coffee.

The warden found me. "I hope it was OK putting the two boys in with you. They weren't too noisy?"

"No, they were good guys. Have they gone?"

"Yes, I think they wanted to see the sunrise."

I could imagine them, two Tiggers bouncing up and down in a lay-by, their first experience of a sunrise that didn't involve staggering out of a nightclub first. I was pleased for them. They were great.

For me, this was a big day. 45 miles, heading properly south, into the hills, into the wind. I needed an early start.

"Are you still coming for breakfast?" Sujir and Anne were packing up to go.

"Um."

"Go on."

"Alright then."

They were very persuasive.

The climb up to the village was hard into the wind, but the views were stunning. Off to the right, beyond the Kyle of Tongue, the ruined Mackay castle perched on a ridge, stark against a blue sky dotted with puffs of white cloud. In the valley southwards, woods and fields led the eye to a series of peaks, one of which must be Ben Loyal, the most northerly of the 'Munros', the over-3,000-foot peaks of Scotland. They were rock-and-grass-covered mountains and – with the woods and trees in front of me – this was very different to the flow country just a few miles to the east.

We breakfasted well in the café attached to the shop / post office, supped our coffee and talked about our routes.

I showed them my map, with Cycle Route One taking me up into the foothills of Ben Loyal, next to Loch Loyal, as far as a first possible stop at The Full Beer Glass seventeen miles away in Altnaharra.

"The hotel in Altnaharra is closed," Anne said.

"Pardon?"

"It's not open. I came that way."

I looked at the map. The next Full Beer Glass was another eight miles further on at Crask.

"Crask is open," Anne said.

So, I had 25 miles before there was anywhere to shelter or get food. Then another 20 miles, though mostly downhill from that point.

"I think I had better get some more food in, then go," I said.

We said goodbye, with Anne setting off back down my route, and Sujir meandering his way around Scotland in his hired car, before setting off back to California.

The road rose very fast out of Tongue, and I moved very slowly, the wind battering me backwards. Before long I was into proper mountain country, with tussocky grass, bracken and purple heather on either side, and Ben Loyal approaching, silhouetted against a sunny blue sky. Skylarks launched themselves out of the heather up into the wind, twittering wildly above me. Loch Loyal came up on my left and the single-track road took to its shores, the wind blowing up surfers' waves on the loch. Beyond the loch were the rounded grassy slopes of Ben Hope, with little shadows of clouds fleeing northwards. Above me on my right was the increasingly precipitous and craggy summit of Ben Loyal. It was fantastic country, beautiful and empty.

I stopped for a drink and spotted that I had a text from Niall. 'Broke down near Loch Lomond. Back wheel bent. Had to walk to town and get lift to shop. Back on road now.' I looked around me. Not a house or even a tree in sight and no cars for some time.

"How's the back wheel, Scott?"

"Straight and true."

"I'm pleased about that."

My cheeks were starting to feel tight with the mix of the wind and the sun, so I dug out the sun screen and made my face look much younger.

At the far end of the loch there were rolling stretches of mountain grasses, and where there were marshy patches or ditches, little yellow and white flowers invisible from a distance. I stopped by a carved stone pillar by the road. It looked new, the lettering picked out in gold: Mackay Country – Fàilte ('welcome' in Gaelic). Goodbye Mackay country, I thought. Over the brow of a hill, with forestry appearing, the road dropped and I whizzed down into Altnaharra.

There were about half a dozen houses, with a lovely little primary school, and a play-area attached. Next to that, were picnic benches, perfect for lunch in the sunshine. I could have done with a break to rest legs really, but with the cold wind, it was not warm enough to linger.

As I cycled on, I could see the hotel off to the left down a hill. Whether it was closed or not, I couldn't tell, but I already had my sights set on the Crask Inn, or as I liked to imagine it, 'The Full Beer Glass of Crask, speciality: Real Ale and Proper Tea'.

High fences guarded the hillside above the road towards TFBGoC. Inside the fences seemed to be natural tree growth, rather than forestry. It felt as though a good attempt was being made to regenerate a highland Scotland before the sheep and deer had eaten any shoots of tree or shrub. Or maybe it was to do with providing shooting. Then again, perhaps it was the landowner who wanted to reintroduce wild animals to the highlands – including wolves. The locals, it was said, were not generally keen.

It felt a long few miles to TFBGoC, and as I swung off the saddle I noticed the average speed on my bike computer for the day – just 8 miles per hour. Very slow, but with the wind and the hills, maybe not too bad.

The Full Beer Glass of Crask, otherwise known as The Crask Inn, was a lonely building, seemingly in the middle of nothing at all. It was a traditional place, with no mod cons, but it had beer, food, shelter, fishing magazines and chat. And that was fine.

"Do you get many cyclists?" I asked the lady minding the bar. Not a busy job in the middle of the day – I was the only customer.

"Yes. On their way to John O'Groats. Had a group of fifty last Friday."

"Did you feed them all?"

"Oh, they're easy to feed. Like fishermen."

"Just … lots of food?"

"Oh yes. Lots. Easy."

She didn't have any lemon drizzle cake, so I was slightly concerned about my Vitamin C levels, but she did have strawberry jam to go with the scones, so at least they were healthy.

Outside, two cyclists appeared. They were Dutch, and had arrived here by way of Germany, Denmark, Sweden, Norway, Shetland and Orkney. But apart from that list, they were very uncommunicative, so I set off.

I was tired now, 25 miles into the wind having some effect. I had hoped from the map that the land would drop away, but I was in a long fairly flat valley, with large tracts of forestry on either side. Areas that had been cut looked devastated, with dead branches everywhere and tree stumps dry and sad. The mature forestry was dense with trees, dark inside a canopy and wall of dark green.

Finally, as the afternoon wore on, the road fell away, and I coasted down to the end of Loch Shin, its blue waters stretching up into the valley beyond. The road ran around the shore until arriving in the village of Lairg. Here there was a shop that sold, amongst other things, energy drinks and chocolate raisins, which was fortunate because that is exactly what I was looking for.

Across a bridge and I was following signs for The Falls of Shin. The road was a gentle downhill through sun-dappled trees above a fast-running river. A sign took me into a car park for the tourist attraction that was The Falls of Shin. It was twenty past five, and tartan-uniformed ladies were closing up the large-looking shop.

"Excuse me, are there toilets here?" I asked.

"They're through the shop," said the lady with a large bunch of keys protruding from the main door. "But I can let you in."

"Really?"

She did just that, and I walked through a darkened store to where more ladies were cleaning the restaurant and who directed me to the toilets. Walking back through, I could see that everything was tastefully expensive, which I suppose is how a Harrods-owned visitor attraction ought to be.

Outside again, and I found signs for mini-golf and forest walks, and also for views over the spectacular falls. I followed the last of these, and the falls were indeed very pretty, with white water surging over rocks and tumbling past the overhanging trees. I watched three fishermen casting hopefully into the fast-moving stream. A lady followed me down the path and stood watching as well.

"Do you think they are after salmon?" I asked.

"It's a bit early," she said, her Scots accent strong. "The salmon will mostly be here from the end of July."

"Do you live here?"

"Not far. I'm just walking. And you're cycling?"

"I am. As far as Carbisdale today."

She nodded, smiling. "You'll like Carbisdale."

I had loved the route altogether today. Starting on the far north coast, up into the mountains, past the wind-swept loch, through forests, and now slipping easily down through wild, broad-leaved woodland, never far from the sparkling, gurgling river. The sun had shone on me all day, though was sliding away towards evening. It had been a long day. A hard day against the wind. I was left feeling tired yet happy with a wonderful day's journey. All it needed was, say, a castle to stay the night in, and the day would be complete.

My little B-road by the river joined a busier main road and I was whizzed over the water and further southwards. Ahead, growing in size as I closed in, was a castle.

I was still following cycle route signs and was taken by surprise when they suddenly pointed me at a railway bridge over the broad, stately river. The bridge was latticed metalwork, the rail line in the centre and a walkway hanging off the side, reached by a short flight of steep steps. The steps and walkway were definitely the route.

"Scott," I said. "Hup!"

"Pardon."

"Hup!!"

Silence.

"Oh, for heaven's sake."

I took the panniers off Scott's rack and lugged them up the steps, went back down and lugged Scott up, then put the panniers back on and picked my way across the precarious walkway above the river.

A drive led through woods, between turreted gateposts and wrought-iron gates into the forecourt of the castle. Immediately ahead stood a tower seven storeys high, also turreted, two arrow slits in a mostly blank stone wall, and a black circle where a clock-face should be. Beyond was an arched entrance to allow the lords and ladies in their horse-driven carriages to be dropped off under cover, and beyond again a large wing of the castle with Victorian-looking windows, and still those turrets on the roof line.

This was Carbisdale Castle. Former home of the Dowager Duchess of Sutherland, and now a Youth Hostel. Fabulous.

The Dowager Duchess of Sutherland was the colourful widow of the man styled the 3rd Duke and 18th Earl of Sutherland. In 1892, the Duke's will left her a vast proportion of his estate, which didn't please his son and heir. A court case saw the Dowager Duchess sent to Holloway Prison for six weeks for destroying documents. Eventually a deal was done. In return for the son receiving a more proportionate amount of the estate, he would pay for a home for his step-mother, built to her specifications. It could be anywhere outside Sutherland. She chose a site above the river here at Culrain in Easter Ross – just outside Sutherland – and in fact dominating the road and rail route into Sutherland. The family would be reminded of the Dowager Duchess every time they travelled south.

This too was the reason for the blank clock face on the tower above me and facing towards Sutherland; the Dowager Duchess 'would not so much as give the Sutherland family the time of day'.

The castle was sold on after the Duchess's death, and in 1945 given to the Scottish Youth Hostel Association.

I leaned Scott against a pillar and went to check in. On the instruction of a smiley young woman behind a very large reception desk, I took Scott round the back of the castle, down a slope and underneath the castle itself into an open undercroft.

85

When I had told my brother Andy that I was coming here, he related a story that he and (another brother) Steve had also cycled here some years before. They had parked their bikes, and instead of returning to the entrance had tried one of the doors from the undercroft. Steps had led them up into an empty wood-panelled room. They had let the door shut behind them and wandered around the room, failing to find a door to go out from. They then realised that the door they came in from had also disappeared, heavily disguised as ordinary wood panelling. Somewhat unsettled, and knowing the castle had a reputation for its ghosts, they tapped their way around the walls, eventually finding a door which led them back down the same steps to their bikes, from where, chastened, they walked round to the proper entrance.

I could see a door at the back of the undercroft.

"What do you think, Scott?"

"It's a door."

"I know it's a door. Should I try it?"

"The last person to do that is probably still trying to tap his way out of that room."

I made my way past junk stacked against the wall and tried the door. It was locked.

"Shame," I said to Scott. "I was up for it."

"You didn't try very hard."

I looked around the undercroft, open to the elements on one side, junk against the walls, cobwebs overhead.

"I think you'll be very comfortable here," I said. "I'll just be in the Dowager Duchess of Sutherland's castle if you're looking for me."

My shin banged on his pedal as I went past.

At the reception desk, I was disappointed to be given a sheet sleeping bag and a key to a dormitory; it seemed unlikely that I would have a four-poster bed.

Doors led through into a magnificent hall dominated by life-size marble statues of mostly naked ladies, their bare bottoms and breasts no doubt proving educational to some of the younger school parties who stayed here. Portraits in gold-leafed frames lined wood-panelled walls. At the far end, a young woman was seated painting a copy of one of the portraits. From the high arched ceiling, brass chandeliers gave a weak light, but showed where a substantial wooden staircase made its way up towards the dormitories. I climbed the stairs, standing to one side for a walking-booted older couple and for two gossipy young girls. From half way up the flight of stairs, I looked back down hall. This was quite extraordinary.

The dormitory was pretty big, with about eight sets of bunk beds spread around the room. Only a few were taken, and I found myself one close to the bay window with its view down over the courtyard.

I did a little tour of the castle after my shower. There were two lounges, each with stuccoed ceilings, whose designer must have had stalactites in mind when he planned them. He? Perhaps it was 'she'. The Dowager Duchess herself? I wouldn't have been surprised. They also had deep comfortable settees and more portraits and landscapes around the walls. Early evening sunshine slanted through tall windows and lit up wide expanses of tartan carpet.

I walked out on to the balcony, and the view up and down the valley from this height was glorious. In one direction, a view through fir trees looked up into forested hills above the river. In the other direction, pink rhododendron heads punctuated the greenery of sun-lit silver birches. These framed the pale whisper of the loch I was heading for tomorrow.

There was a canteen, and I was served next to a young guy.

"Do you mind if I join you?" he asked, when I had sat myself at a table.

"Please."

David was from Edinburgh, travelling by himself to see something of a Scotland he had never visited.

"Perth was the furthest north I'd been," he said, shaking his head.

"So you're just driving wherever suits you?"

"No, not driving. I'm going by train. That's part of it as well."

"And meeting people along the way?"

He grinned. "I am that."

He was an amiable guy in his mid-twenties, just without friends who would enjoy train journeys into the highlands, and staying in youth hostels along the way, taking pot luck with sheet sleeping bags, dormitories and marble-statued castles.

"How are you travelling?" he asked me.

"Cycling."

"Hey," he said. "Hey, that's good." He looked very thoughtful. "That's really good."

Captain's log: Day Five

Target:	45.0 miles	72.0 Km
Actual distance:	47.7 miles	76.3 Km
Average speed:	9.7 mph	15.5 Kmph
Maximum speed:	24.5 mph	39.2 Kmph
Total distance:	188.8 miles	302.1 Km

I was woken late that night in the dark dormitory by snoring. I suspected it might have been me.

Across the room, someone turned over.

Day Six

**Target: 47 miles / 75.2Km
From Carbisdale Castle to the Black Isle
via the Glenmorangie Distillery
and the Cromarty Firth**

I woke early, with light poking in past the curtains, and snuck a look out. The sun was shining and the trees were still. Astonishingly there was no wind.

I made my way down the staircase and out into the courtyard. It was true. There really was no wind. After five days of what had felt like constant wind in my face, the day was calm and sunny. I decided to celebrate by having breakfast at a picnic bench in the courtyard.

Although I had been up early, time slipped away as I enjoyed just sitting in the warmth of the morning. A family packed up a minibus with rucksacks and sleeping bags and drove off. An older guy fitted 30-year-old panniers to his bike and 70-year-old feet into pedals and set off down the drive.

I looked at my map. It was to be another long day. 47 miles, 75 kilometres. Down the valley, along the coast past Tain, across the entrance to the Cromarty Firth by way of the Nigg Ferry, to my bed-and-breakfast on the Black Isle. The route was more down than up. Certainly no mountains today. So I took my time, not realising then what was to come later that day.

Having collected Scott, I took a last look back at the castle.

"The castle was good, Scott," I said. "You'd have liked it in there."

"You had a four-poster bed, I assume?"

"Well, no."

"Not much of a castle then."

"Well –"

David came out. He had a small rucksack on his back and a timetable in his hand.

"So this is the bike?"

"Scott," I said.

"Scott?"

"Scott."

"And you'll cycle this –"

"Scott."

"You'll cycle Scott right the way across Scotland?"

"That's the plan."

He poked a finger at the sticky tape arrangement on the panniers designed to stop mud flicking up over me. He also cast an eye over the dirt-spattered frame. And at the front pannier held on by cable-ties.

"Mm. I'd better get my train. Well, take care."

We set off, a bit faster than David's walking pace, and I waved as we rounded the corner.

"Not everyone appreciates you like I do, Scott," I said.

"I am thankful for small mercies."

The drive joined a country road bordered by hedgerows with pink foxgloves and yellow broom springing out of them. We wound through woods above the river, which soon broadened out into a loch, with green-coated hills beyond. It was fabulous cycling.

After a few miles the road ran into the village of Ardgay. The road here had once been the main route north, crossing the Dornoch Firth to the village of Bonar Bridge on the other side of the waters. Now there was a modern bridge further down, with the fast A9 speeding traffic northwards and missing Ardgay completely. The village had a lost, abandoned air.

We shadowed the coast of the Dornoch Firth and also the railway line I had travelled north on a week before. The cycling was completely flat with only long slow curves as it kept to the lochside. To begin with, this was fine. But after another five miles or so, I got to thinking that a café would be good. Since there was no sign of one and the map had not shown even half a beer glass, I stopped in a gateway to a field, admired the foxgloves, ate a muesli bar, had a drink, and set off again.

After another five miles I reached the houses that make up Edderton. No shop. No café.

"How's the Vitamin C level?" Scott asked.

"Could be better."

Another three miles and the main A9 bridge loomed.

The bridge brought traffic from the north in on to my quiet road, and suddenly my quiet road was a major road, without a cycle path along side. All I had was the gap between grass and white line. Two miles of it was enough, and I gratefully pulled off at the turn into the village of Tain, and even more gratefully into the car park of the Glenmorangie Distillery.

The car park overlooked the stone-built distillery building, with its sash windows and red doors. To the left, the roof of an adjoining building had the distinctive pagoda-style roof of the whisky distilling room.

Glenmorangie, according to the Malt Whisky Companion, had a House-style that was '*Creamy, leafy. Restorative or with dessert,*' and a 10-year-old malt whose Palate was '*Spicy, flowery, and malty sweet tones that are creamy, almost buttery. A suggestion of bananas*?'. It was the best-selling malt whisky in Scotland, and its distillery was the first open one on my journey.

I looked seriously at Scott. "I may be gone some time."

Wide doors stood open to display 'The Still House'. The ground floor was disinfectantly clean, with a paved floor, tiled circular vats and stainless steel pipework. The eyes were drawn immediately upwards and here it was totally different – more like a cathedral than a distillery.

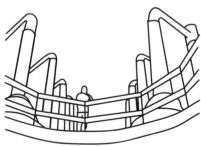

The high wood-slatted ceiling had large windows in the roof, through which light streamed down on to what looked like wide organ pipes, stretching up towards the roof. They were made of polished brass, wider at the bottom, narrowing as they rose towards the light – the famous still-pipes of Glenmorangie, the tallest in Scotland.

A lumberjack-shirted man stood on the balcony with his back to me, studying something he was holding. I had no doubt that he was one of the Sixteen Men Of Tain, the privileged few who create Glenmorangie whisky.

Opposite the doors to the Still House was the visitor centre. A central counter housed two ladies dealing with the purchasing needs of a group of middle-aged Germans who were either circulating around the cabinets against each wall, or filing out with their sets of glasses or their boxed bottles. I too roamed the wall cabinets.

Each cabinet was devoted to a variation on the Glenmorangie Whisky theme. There were big bottles, smaller bottles and miniatures. There were the 10-year-old, the 18-year-old and even the 25-year-old. I had expected different sizes of bottles and different ages of maturity, but there was more here. There were different flavours based on maturing the whisky in barrels previously used to hold madeira, or port, or bourbon, or sherry, or sauterne. The attention to detail was amazing. Glenmorangie actually own woodland in Kentucky, from which they produce barrels to lend to a bourbon producer for four years, before shipping them back to Tain. And they only use the trees from one side of the hill because they are more absorbent. I was mesmerised. Had I been travelling by car, I might have emerged with a large-ish bottle. Maybe several. As it was, I approached the counter and bought a miniature.

I should have felt disappointed, but in fact I felt triumphant.

"Scott," I said, when I had returned to the car park. "Look. My first."

"So how is that going to help with the Vitamin C deficiency?"

"……… the Vitamin C deficiency."

We cycled on into Tain to find lunch. Tain was just a small town but it had a wide-ish main street and some surprisingly grand buildings with, at roof level, little round turrets. Flags were strung across the main street, and there were tiered baskets of flowers. There was also a good sprinkling of shops, enough to supply me with sandwiches and a coffee anyway.

I pottered into the Church of St Duthus, not a saint I had heard of, but apparently one whose relics brought thousands of pilgrims to the town before the reformation. I learned more in 'Tain Through Time', a little museum across the other side of the churchyard. I mooched quietly through Tain's past – the pilgrims, the visits from the King, the silversmiths, the airforce base with its Polish pilots. It was really quite pleasant. Not exciting perhaps. But pleasant.

"Scott," I said, when I was back at the bike. "Tain is pleasant."

"Not exciting then?"

"No. Pleasant."

Once out of Tain, my Cycle Route One map took me out into countryside along quiet and flat lanes. The sun was shining, and every now and then, a little cycle route sign pointed me in the right direction. Away off to the left was the Dornoch Firth. Ahead of me, eastwards and out of sight for the moment, was the sea.

I seemed to be cycling through what had been the old airforce base. Occasional military buildings appeared – concrete block-houses and corrugated iron roofs, abandoned long ago. It must have been a huge base, and I wondered what the Polish flyers had made of Tain. I wondered if some had stayed, another shot of new blood in the Scottish arm.

At the wonderfully named Hilton of Cadboll, we reached the sea and the road swung southwards. Bungalows with neatly trimmed gardens looked out across the sea to a long horizon bearing two tiny tankers heading slowly north. Then I was out in the countryside again – grain fields mostly – and looking very productive. It was all so extraordinarily different to my day in the hills and along the north coast. It felt a different world. It felt almost southern, which of course it had no right to do; I was a day north of Inverness and still had the Cairngorms to cross before dropping down into the urban world of central Scotland.

My bike computer had just clicked up 30 miles for the day when I cycled past a church in the little village of Nigg and my eye caught a sign for 'The Nigg Stone'. I left Scott by the gate to the churchyard and made my way into the church. It was small, simple and quiet, T-shaped with a pulpit in the centre of the T. The walls were whitewashed, with nothing to distract a congregation's attention from a minister in the pulpit. Nothing could be more different from the other church I had been in a few days before – the Italian Chapel on Orkney, with its brilliantly painted walls, its altar and its wrought-iron screen. A quite distinctive Christianity had built this church, and through in an adjoining room, another sort of Christianity was represented.

The Nigg Stone was around 1300 years old, carved for the picts after their conversion to Christianity. It stood over two metres high and was about half a metre across. Carved into the sandstone to almost the full height of the stone was a giant Celtic cross. There were stone swirls, circles and intertwined snakes. In the triangular piece at the top were carved animals. I moved around the back, and here there were more carvings. Some maybe biblical, some maybe of 'the pictish beast', which apparently appears on a good few stones.

Between this mysterious Celtic Christianity from an almost unknown past, the deeply Roman Catholic Italian Chapel constructed in the midst of war, and the Presbyterian plain-ness here based around the bible, it pressed on me how many ways the Christian message had been interpreted.

My goal was the Nigg ferry which would nip me across the mouth of the Dornoch Firth to the Black Isle beyond. The

Black Isle was an odd name, since it was neither an island nor particularly black. In fact, it was a peninsula, and was likely to be more green than black, judging by the map. By nipping across I could save cycling all the way around the Cromarty Firth, and instead cycle direct to my bed-and-breakfast at Avoch, just beyond Fortrose part way down the Black Isle. From there, I would have a shorter day into Inverness the day after – a rest day.

"You have," Scott said, "phoned to check the sailing times?"

"Not... as such," I said.

"Checked that it is running at all?"

"Well, I'm sure it will be."

Silence.

"Look," I said, "the website said that the 'Cromarty Rose' can take 50 people and two cars. It's a proper ferry."

Silence.

"It probably just goes to and fro all the time."

Silence.

"It'll be fine."

The road dropped down to sea level and here there were warehouses and oil storage sites, but some of them were quiet to the point of not actually being open any more. Little blue Route One signs took me past them, and finally the land ran out and here was the ferry terminal.

I knew it was the ferry terminal, because there was a jetty sticking out into the water and a little blue Route One sign pointing at it. Off to the left was open sea. Off to the right was the long bay of the Dornoch Firth. Straight ahead, across about half a mile of water, was the Black Isle. There was also a large sign which said, 'Ferry departs every half hour, 08.15 – 18.15'.

There was also another sign showing fares and operating details. Unfortunately, this had a big red cross going through it. There was also a blue nylon rope tied across the entrance ramp.

Another small clue to there being a problem was that the

whole place looked completely abandoned. There were no cars. No people. And quite clearly no ferry.

"So it's fine then?" Scott said.

"Um."

"I may have mentioned this before, but you can be a blithering idiot sometimes."

"I don't think you've mentioned that before."

"You just weren't listening."

On the other side of the car park, a long white building had the word 'Hotel' quite prominently displayed. I walked over to see if I could get some more information. A notice was taped to the door: 'This is a private house. The hotel is in receivership.'

"Ah."

I went back to Scott and pulled out the map. If I had to cycle all the way around the Dornoch Firth, it looked as though it would add about 30 miles to today's ride. I had already ridden 35 miles. With lightening speed I calculated that I would therefore be cycling 65 miles today.

I phoned my friend, Ian, and told him of my predicament. When he had stopped laughing, he told me that I had made his day.

"Thank you for your support," I said.

"So you didn't phone to check then?"

"I – "

A car pulled around in front of the hotel. Or rather, the private house.

"Ian, I'll phone you back."

I ran across to where the lady was going inside.

"Hello," I said. "Can you tell me, is the ferry running?"

"Broke down yesterday."

"Oh. So it's not going to run today?"

"No. Not today."

"Ah."

She closed the door on me.

Not going to run today.

65 miles.

I walked back over to Scott.

"Scott," I said. "I am an idiot."

"I may have mentioned that."

I checked the map again. I would have to cycle north (north! aaghh!), then loop around the top of the Firth, then down the west coast, joining the horrid A9, cross the A9 road bridge, then cycle north again (north! aaghh!) to Avoch. It could easily be more than 65 miles for the day.

"Balderdash," I said, though again that might not have been my exact phrasing.

Back at what I had taken to be an abandoned warehouse, a security guard was reading his paper in a little hut. I cycled over.

"The ferry," I said. "Is it not running?"

"Broke down yesterday."

"Balderdash," I said. Probably.

So I cycled north, then west, then south, and for some while it was really nice cycling. The roads were B-roads or lanes and they had hardly any traffic. They took me through quiet farmland with hedgerows and cows. Off to the west were hills, grey in a light haze. Above me, the sun shared a mid-blue sky with puffy clouds.

I stopped being cross with myself.

For a while.

I wasn't sure what Scott was thinking.

At Milton I joined what must originally have been the main road, but which now rolled me easily along the coast towards Invergordon.

This had been a vast naval area until fifty years ago. When the fleet was in, naval ships would have welcomed this deep-water shelter and the town of Invergordon would have been overflowing with servicemen.

I was cycling next to the water, which looked calm, dark and deep. In fact it must have been really deep, because ahead of me was a very large ship moored off-shore. Across the water, about three or four miles away, was the Black Isle. Still tantalisingly close, and quite, quite inaccessible.

As I got closer the ship turned into a cruise liner. I pulled in at a little car park not far from where a long jetty reached out to meet the liner. A couple of cars were parked, their owners standing at the low wall above a rocky beach taking photographs of the ship.

From the pointy end (a technical term), the ship sloped up to the bridge with its large wrap-around windows. Behind that there was an open deck. I counted seven rows of windows from there down to the water-line, where blue curvey waves had been painted against the white of the vessel. Smoke curled away gently from the sloping funnel above the blunt end (another technical term).

Bagpipe music drifted across from the cruise ship, and I imagined there was a welcoming band aboard.

I also imagined myself cycling out across the jetty. After all, here was a ship. I wanted to get just across some water.

"Scott," I said, "do you think if I offered the captain £5 he would take me across the other side?"

"Probably not."

"£10?"

"I suspect," he said, "that they have certain standards."

It was getting on in the afternoon, and I was hungry. I cycled up into Invergordon's town centre, which seemed a bustly place. There were plenty of shops on either side of a wide main street, some with fabulous murals painted on them – a lifeboat, the loch, fishermen. I poked my head into a café and found the owner sweeping up.

"Are you still serving food?"

He looked at his watch.

"Well, I could do some sandwiches."

"Wonderful."

Actually, he did enormous sandwiches.

I asked about the cruise ship. It was one of the smaller ones that docked here now, with maybe 1,300 passengers.

The bigger ones had around 2,300.

"Plus, there might be 400 crew. Not all of them come ashore, but enough do to bring trade into the town."

"So, do the passengers go into Inverness?"

"There are coach trips organised. Inverness, Culloden, Loch Ness. There are due to be 53 cruise liners come in this year. When I first came here, there were four."

"Where are you from?"

"Swindon."

"This isn't like Swindon."

He smiled.

"Not much."

It was already late on in the afternoon and I probably had twenty miles still to cycle.

I phoned the bed-and-breakfast before I left Invergordon.

"It's going to be at least another two hours, maybe three, before I get to Avoch," I said to the lady who answered the phone.

"It's Och," she said.

"Och?"

"Yes, the locals call it Och, not Avoch."

"Oh. Well, at least a couple of hours."

"No problem. We're just here."

I checked the map. I had a B-road for a while, but after that I would have no choice. It would have to be the A9, and the little I had seen of that had already scared me. Unless I was prepared to cycle even further around the loch, rather than take the A9 bridge, I would have to brave it. Still, there would probably be a cycle lane or at least a wide bit to the left of the white line at the side of the road. Surely.

I used parallel roads where I could, and that helped for a few miles, but finally, I had to join the A9. I pulled up at a junction, first having to cross over traffic coming the other way.

It took a while before there was a gap in the traffic. Then I was over, and waiting at the other side for a gap for me to slip into. That took a while as well.

I finally pulled out on to the road when a slow lorry was holding up the faster traffic. It soon caught me though, and coughed and belched past, exhaust fumes flowing over me. I tried to hold my breath till it was gone. When it had passed, I put my head down and cycled as fast as I could, every few seconds conscious of a car, van or lorry rumbling past me far too close. I cycled on the left of the white line, trying to avoid rubbish and stones flicked there by the traffic. I had to concentrate hard to avoid meandering into the path of the latest vehicle to rush past me. Perhaps it was the time of day, or perhaps I was just unlucky with the volume of traffic, or perhaps I was just too slow to set a decent pace. Either way, it was awful.

After a few miles the road split and I followed signs for the bridge. The bridge, if anything, was worse. The lanes were narrow, and there was no gap between the white line and the side of the road. I found myself intently cycling on the white line itself, scared all the time that the next wing mirror would catch me and fling me to the floor with those huge wheels thundering towards me. I can tell you nothing about the bridge, or the view from it. My eyes were so firmly fixed on that white line, trying not to deviate by an inch.

At the far side I was finally able to pull off the main road. I stopped in a lay-by and took my hands off the handle-bars. I could hardly believe the tension in them.

"Scott," I said. "Let's not do that again."

"I don't know why we did it in the first place. Why did you phone the lady in Avoch and tell her we were going to be late? Why didn't you say we wouldn't make it, and we could have stayed somewhere else?"

I looked up at the large hill rising ahead of us.

"It's Och, not Avoch," I said.

A lane took us up a rise into the village of Culboken. It wasn't really that much of a rise, I suppose, but it had been a long way, and my panniers were getting heavier.

101

At a T-junction, I pondered going left then right to cross the ridge, or right then left. A lady with a shopping bag appeared.

"Excuse me," I said. "Which is the best road to Avoch?"

"Och," she said. "Right then left, left again then keep going up the hill."

I thanked her, turned right, then left, then left and kept going up the hill.

By half way, I was struggling for breath and my legs were starting to burn. I got off and just managed to avoid throwing Scott into a ditch.

Looking back though, I could see down to the A9 bridge where it crossed the Cromarty Firth. Beyond that, forest skirted the lower slopes of mountains which seemed to flow into the distance, still with patches of snow in nooks and crannies.

I ploughed on up the hill, into forest towards the top of the ridge, then we were going down, and it was so, so good, if over far, far too soon. We turned on to another A-road, but this one was quiet, and it rolled down, up and down into Avoch.

Och.

I checked the bike computer.

70.4 miles.

Not the 45 planned.

The bed-and-breakfast was a bungalow on the edge of the town. As I was almost coming to expect, the owners were English. They signed me in and pointed me at the shower.

I walked into Avoch to find somewhere to eat. Avoch looked as though it had been a fishing village, with its quay and its whitewashed rows of cottages looking out across trimmed grass to the sea. The harbour now held sailing and motor boats, rather than fishing boats. It was pretty, but just a bit quiet. In fact, there was nobody around at all to see me stumble off a pavement and tweek my ankle. I sat down a moment rubbing it, wondering whether I should have heeded the advice from my physiotherapist that I needed to do exercises to strengthen my ankles.

I pottered into the restaurant of a hotel. It was a big room, and was totally empty apart from me. After several minutes standing at the bar looking for someone who I could order food from, a face finally poked through the doorway.

I ate scampi and chips alone, and wondered why on earth I had cycled so far to be here.

Captain's log: Day Six

Target:	45.0 miles	72.0 Km
Actual distance:	70.4 miles	112.6 Km
Average speed:	12.2 mph	19.5 Kmph
Maximum speed:	29.0 mph	46.4 Kmph
Total distance:	259.2 miles	414.7 Km

I phoned Claire at home. The reception was rubbish.

Day Seven

Target: 19 miles / 30.4Km
From the Black Isle to Inverness
via Chanonry Point

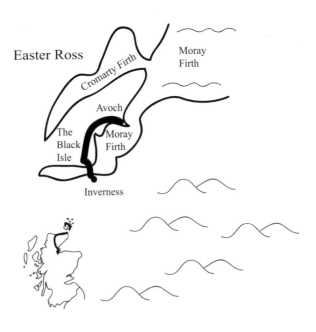

The 'Nature'. That was what I needed.

We headed north from Avoch, in the wrong direction for Inverness. We cycled through the little town of Fortrose, past the Co-op and the dark sandstone ruins of Fortrose Cathedral, and turned right at a sign for Chanonry Point.

A small road led through a golf course, bounded by the sea on both sides, as the triangle of Chanonry Point narrowed to its, well, point. It was a Friday morning, misty and murky, and grey-haired golfers were dinking balls on to greens just a short distance from the water. There must be an awful lot of golf balls lost here. There certainly would be if I were to try my hand, anyway.

I didn't play golf, but I had to admit this was quite a place. I'd read on an American website that this was many golfers' favourite course, and I could see why. Rolling, close-cropped fairways made their way past the yellow and green of gorse, via fiendish little sand traps, and on to even closer cropped greens with little flag-poles bisecting a view across the Moray Firth to the blue foothills of the mountains beyond.

The road finished close to the end of the narrowing spit of land. The clubhouse stood on one side. On the other, a white-painted lighthouse rose to a cross-glazed bubble of glass and a dark circular roof. The lighthouse was protected from the nearby water with a sandstone wall, and a couple were just setting off past it along the pebble, sand and seaweed beach. Beyond them, about twenty people were standing at the water's edge.

"Scott," I said. "Wait here."

"Here?"

"It's the Nature," I said.

As I made my way across the beach towards the group, a dark shape leapt gracefully out of the water beyond them, and slipped just as gracefully back beneath the waves. It was a dolphin.

Then there was another. And another. A thin snout would lead the way, a dark curved fin following, and then the wide flipper of a tail.

As I joined the people at the shoreline, cameras clicked around me, little children exclaimed, and I said, "Blow me."

Now there were two or three dolphins leaping at once. I looked around. Several men had cameras with foot-long lenses on tripods. I took out my little camera and felt slightly foolish. The dolphins seemed to deserve more than my efforts to capture them, each time ending with a photo of a disappearing tail.

But the photos were also somehow irrelevant. It was the being there that was important, watching the dolphins cavort in the water so close to the shore.

Suddenly one leapt in a most uncoordinated and ungraceful way, crashing back on to the water, spray flying up. That one, I thought, had just caught lunch.

I stood watching the dolphins for about ten minutes amongst the line of people along the shore, then moved back up the beach slightly so as to take in the whole scene.

A lady was sitting on a blanket with her little scottie dog. She seemed to be people-watching rather than dolphin-watching.

"Amazing," I said.

"Aren't they? Have you not seen them before?"

"No."

"We come here as often as we can. My husband is down there. In fact, we sponsor one of the dolphins. Nevis."

"Nevis?"

"He has a white tip on the end of his fin. Like snow on the top of Ben Nevis."

"Excellent."

"Nevis is out there today."

"So why are they here? Sorry, my name's Mike. I'm just, sort of, cycling."

"I'm Julie. Well, when the tide comes in, it meets the river just here, stirs it up, and the fish come to feed. Salmon and trout and so on. And that attracts the bottle-nosed dolphins and the seals. There are some seals just around the point the other way."

"They are fantastic to watch."

"We saw a group of around fifty here once. Only a few people used to know about the spot, but it's been on Spring Watch on the telly, so now you get lots."

"And you, where have you come from?"

"The Wirral. We used to come up here and walk with the dog, but he's fifteen now, so we cycle with him in a kiddie-seat on the back."

"And you come here to watch the dolphins."

"Yes," she said, and her eyes strayed down to the shore again, no doubt keeping a look out for Nevis.

I wondered if Nevis was keeping a look out for Julie.

The road was up and down as I cycled back southwards again. The sun burned off the murky cloud at little Munlochy and I stopped at a viewpoint by the main road, a bench proving far too inviting. Today, I thought, was a rest-day, just a couple of hours cycling, with time for watching dolphins, and time for doing some clothes-washing and shopping for provisions in Inverness this afternoon. So I rested and took in the scene.

The view towards and beyond the Moray Firth was beguiling. The arm of the sea turned gentle blue as the clouds above rolled away, and I could see across to the wooded hills beyond Inverness. One of those hills would be Culloden, last resting place of many of the clansmen who followed Bonnie Prince Charlie.

Munlochy's Clootie Well was just a couple of miles away, right next to the road. A Forestry Commission sign read, 'Hope hangs in the branches', and every branch within hand's reach held some piece of clothing or rag tied to it – the 'cloots'. Older cloots had greyed and weathered; newer ones were bright white or yellow or red, even rainbow-coloured blankets and cloths, lively T-shirts with children's designs, cloths with messages hand-written and fading. Every one, it seemed, represented a wish or a hope for happiness or for health. There was sadness in some, determination in others, desperation in a few. There were hundreds, right up the slope above the road through the trees. Water spilled out of the well itself, a basin set in the earth, and trickled down towards the road amongst the collection of hopes.

When I set off, I sailed past pretty fields and little copses of woodland, cutting across a little headland so that the sea was out of sight. It was lovely countryside. The 'black' isle was certainly not black that day.

At North Kessock the arm of the sea that is the Moray Firth reappeared suddenly, straight ahead of me, as Cycle Route One dropped me down to the shore.

North Kessock was a sleepy place, once the northerly point for the ferries from the 'Capital of the Highlands', which lay in the sunshine across on the far side of the water. Today the village was overshadowed by the North Kessock Bridge way above, with its dull roar of traffic from the A9 on its way to and from Inverness.

I sat by the old slipway, the suspension bridge above and to the left. Houses and bungalows nestled into the wooded hillside behind. There were the usual small-town shops, but also a maker of Jacobite shields: leather-covered with a spike in the front, and beautifully made.

I watched the flow of the tide running past the quayside. North Kessock was another place where dolphins congregated, so I kept an eye out for Nevis's mates. Just now though, there were none to be seen.

A steep cycleway led me breathlessly up on to the bridge, high above the water with long views down to the Firth and over to Inverness and the hills behind. I thought I could see the outlet of the Caledonian Canal, the waterway that cuts across Scotland from north-east to south-west via the Great

Glen and Loch Ness. For another trip, that might be a good ride. Not this one though. I was heading for the Cairngorms.

The bridge had a cycleway, and it was a good feeling, scampering along safely in the sun, no worries about the traffic thundering along just a little way away. I liked this bridge.

I stopped at where I thought was halfway across and pulled out my camera. It took five attempts holding the camera out at arm's length to get a photo that included my whole face rather than a small section of it. At least I had a grin on my face by then.

Below, the white sail of a yacht breezed along the Firth towards me, disappearing beneath the roadway far below.

I rolled down the far side heading towards the town. Route One signs took me through a trading estate and into back streets, where I ran out of signs. I did a couple of loops round busy streets, before finding a policeman who pointed me towards the Tourist Information Centre for the possibility of a map that would guide me to my hostel.

It became clear that Inverness was a real city. The main shopping streets were wide and busy. Some had been pedestrianised, and locals and tourists mingled amongst the first major chain-stores of the journey. There was a robust, no-nonsense feel to the city. I wasn't so sure about the big new shopping centre with a usual mix of Britain's clothes shops and fast-food outlets. It was enclosed, weather-free, and entirely atmosphere-free. It might have been Basildon or Birmingham, Cardiff or Glasgow. I remembered Jen on the train home to Thurso. She must have loved it.

Across a road I spotted the Tourist Information Centre in a modern concrete building up a flight of steps. On my side of the road, a giant Scotsman was extracting leaflets from a pannier on a bike parked in a cycle-rack. I could tell he was a Scot, because he was wearing a kilt, sporran, black jacket, frilly shirt and long socks.

I chained Scott in the rack next to the man's bike.

"Just talk amongst yourselves," I said, and followed the kilted giant over the road.

He was now standing part way up the steps, leaflets in hand, declaiming to the world. This was no ordinary Scot in a kilt. This was a man who would lead you through the streets of Inverness and tell you its history, show you its sights, and generally entertain and amuse you. What's more, he had arrived on a bike, which given his kilt, was extremely brave.

"Tell me," I said, "how does your kilt stay in place when you're cycling?"

The big man turned crinkled eyes on me. "That's what the sporran's for," he said. "It shows the ladies just enough to get them interested, if you take my meaning."

"I do."

I declined his invitation to join a tour, but I am pretty certain that he would be both entertaining and amusing, even if more of his attention was paid to the female members of his tours than to the men.

My hostel was only a short ride away, and a young woman with an accent that I couldn't place welcomed me in. She was around twenty, with shoulder-length brown hair and a broad smile.

"I'm Kirsty," she said.

"Mike," I said.

I made a guess that her accent was Irish, but I was wrong. "Where are you from, Kirsty?"

"From the north coast," she said.

"I've just come from there. Whereabouts?"

"Bettyhill."

"Hey, I liked Bettyhill."

"I'd love to move back one day."

"Is it not that easy?"

"No, there are no jobs there. I could really only move back if I had a business there. And I haven't."

"Maybe one day?"

"Oh, yes," she said, and she grinned. "I hope so. After I've travelled."

This was more of a travellers' hostel than a cyclists' or walkers'. Scott had to be left in the garden chained to a drainpipe, rather than in a shed. He was not impressed.

Kirsty was chatting with a mother and daughter sitting in the lounge / eating area, when I went back in. A TV showing tennis was tucked away in a corner, as was a computer, which, she said, had internet access. There was a kitchen and a shower room, and she gave me a key to a dormitory. No, there were no washing machines, but there was a launderette down the hill.

I was the first occupant of a small dormitory with two double bunks, and I chose the prime spot, the bottom bunk, just behind the door.

Kirsty's directions to the launderette took me past the castle. Not a real castle, not any more, but an imposing red-sandstone council building with a bronze statue outside of Flora MacDonald. Flora had been the saviour of Bonnie Prince Charlie when he escaped across to the Western Isles. Her bronze had turned green with age. The sun shone on Gaelic wording underneath. Translated into English, it read, 'The preserver of Prince Charles Edward Stuart will be mentioned in history and if courage and fidelity be virtues, mentioned with honour.' Yes, I was close now to Culloden.

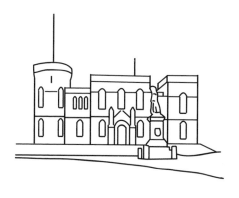

Across a bridge over the wide river Ness, the launderette was full of locals who knew each other, jokes flying across the room amongst the spins and tumbles. I went food-shopping whilst my clothes became more civilised, and returned to the hostel with sweeter smelling clothes and a ready-meal for the hostel's microwave.

It was just after five and I took my meal into the garden to eat. The sun was warming a bench that had a view across roofs to church and cathedral, over the city and to hills in the distance. Flora, I thought, had been looking in that direction, her bronze arm raised to keep the sun from her eyes.

A cyclist brought his bike through to the garden and another drainpipe found an alternative use. Simon was in his mid-thirties, tall and very fit-looking in lycra bike gear. His bike looked a bit fitter than Scott as well. I suspect it didn't have a name.

Simon was followed into the garden by a lady of a similar age, her hexagonal glasses framed by long brown hair. She made to sit on the grass, but Simon and I made room on the bench. Lara was German, she told us in excellent English, and not a cyclist, but a traveller. We compared journeys. Simon was on the start of a cycle-tour of the western highlands, travelling fast and light, cycling 60-80 miles a day. He showed us the pack he had of his entire washing and medical kit. It was about the size of a paperback book. A small one. I guessed his spare clothes would fit into something similar.

"And you?" Lara asked me. "Do you do that?"

"I'm afraid not," I said. "I cycle about half the distance Simon does, but I stop and look at things."

"I would as well."

"I saw dolphins today. In the sea. They were fantastic."

"And tomorrow?"

"Tomorrow, I'm cycling to Culloden and to some stone-age tombs just beyond, and then on to my next hostel in the Cairngorms."

"What is Culloden?"

"Ah, well, Culloden is a battle-field. Have you heard of Bonnie Prince Charlie?"

"I think so."

"Culloden was the battle where Bonnie Prince Charlie was defeated," I said.

Lara nodded and said, "I am not so sure what to do tomorrow."

She had been travelling with three friends, and had wanted to visit Inverness, but her friends had intended to go walking. So she had caught the bus here by herself.

"Well," I said. "I can recommend the dolphins. I guess you can get a bus there from Inverness. Or you could go to Culloden, of course. I'll be there later on in the morning, if you wanted to meet up."

"I would like that."

Kirsty had come out into the garden for a smoke. "I'll find you a bus timetable," she said.

Captain's log: Day Seven

Target:	19.0 miles	30.4 Km
Actual distance:	20.9 miles	33.4 Km
Average speed:	10.0 mph	16.0 Kmph
Maximum speed:	27.0 mph	43.2 Kmph
Total distance:	280.1 miles	448.1 Km

So I was in Inverness, the Capital of the Highlands, seemingly far, far north still, with the Cairngorm mountains still to cross, and then Stirling and Edinburgh and the Southern Uplands.

In cycling days though, I was half way.

And that, I thought as I dozed in my bunk, was encouraging.

Part Two

Inverness
to the Border

Day Eight

Target: 21 miles / 33.6 Km
From Inverness to Tomatin
via Culloden and Clava Cairns

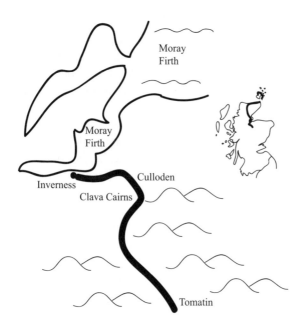

With my eyes closed, standing on one leg, whilst cleaning my teeth, I fell over.

"Morning."

"Oh. Hi, Simon."

"You alright?"

"Fine."

The physiotherapist had been quite specific about that particular exercise to strengthen my ankle. She should perhaps have mentioned doing it when alone.

Lara and I met in the kitchen. I was in no rush again today. This was the second of my rest days, designed to allow legs to recover and time to see the sights, finishing the day at Tomatin Distillery ('*Malty, spicy, rich. Restorative after dinner*') in the fringes of the Cairngorm Mountains. I hadn't mentioned the Cairngorms (or the distillery) to Scott just yet. I also hadn't mentioned that my route through the Cairngorms would have daily mileages of 41, 42, 44 and 51. There were long days to come through the mountains.

I finished writing some postcards and walked into town with Lara, me to the post office, Lara for a bus to Chanonry Point. I would meet her at Culloden Visitor Centre at lunch time.

I got lost cycling out of Inverness.

It was daft really. I had a new map to follow: Cycle Route 7, the northern part of the 'Lochs and Glens' route, and there would be the little blue Sustrans signs to follow. I just couldn't find any of them.

Directions finally took me on a B-road up out of town, where I came across route-signs. The day was warming up and I pedalled easily along country lanes and then through villages and housing estates, before I was suddenly facing one of the most beautiful houses I had seen.

Through wide gates and across a striped emerald lawn, an elegant Georgian building stood four-square. The main part of the building was coated in ivy, the greenery broken up by white-painted sash windows, and by a red carpet climbing the broad steps to an open front door. On either side of the main building were two smaller wings exactly proportioned with the other. In fact, the proportions of the whole building were absolutely perfect. The house would have sat perfectly well in Bath or in Oxford.

A sign said, 'Culloden House' and it was clearly a hotel well beyond my means. Later I checked the website. The cheapest room would have been twelve times the cost of the backpackers hostel. The most expensive suite would have been twenty-five times the cost. Mind you, it would have had a Bose music system, a complimentary laptop computer and a turndown service.

"I suppose we could have stayed here last night, Scott."

"You'd have probably left me in the cellar."

"True."

Culloden House (before the Georgian additions) had been used by Bonnie Prince Charlie before the battle of Culloden and I wondered if he had had an inkling of the disaster that he would bring on Scotland the following day.

In 1688 the Catholic King James (VII of Scotland and II of England) had been ousted from the British throne by the Protestant parliament in London. In 1715 a rising in Scotland in James's favour was defeated, and in 1745, a second Jabobite rising against the German-speaking King George was initiated by the arrival in Scotland of James's son Charles Stuart, 'Bonnie Prince Charlie', the 'Young Pretender'.

He landed on the west coast of Scotland, gradually drawing support from many of the clans – MacDonalds, Grants, Camerons, Macleans and more. But not all. Amongst the list of those opposing him were the Campbells, the most powerful of the clans, and the Sinclairs. Yes, if I had a Scottish ancestor involved in the '45, he would probably have been fighting amongst King George's redcoats, not amongst the Jacobite clansmen.

The Jacobites had moved south through Scotland, taking

the major cities without a great deal of resistance, then marched into England. Through Carlisle and Manchester, they arrived in Derby in December. But Englishmen were not rising to his support in any numbers, support from France had not materialised, and King George's armies were mustering and blocking the way to London. The Jacobite leadership decided on a retreat to Scotland. They managed to avoid battle as they withdrew to Glasgow, then Stirling, then Inverness. All the time though, King George's son, the Duke of Cumberland, was bringing the redcoat army closer.

After a botched night attack on Cumberland, Charles and the Jacobites formed up on Culloden Moor – up on the hill above where I was taking in the serene view of Culloden House.

I cycled up through woodland, which ended as I reached the plateau, then down to the recently built Visitor Centre.

The building was a sleek-lined construction of stone, wood and glass. I left Scott in a bike rack by the fairly full car park, and settled myself in the café with a tea and a piece of carrot cake to top up my Vitamin B levels. It would certainly be one of my five-a-day today.

It was busy. There were families, groups of friends and coach-parties. Scots, English, American, European, though none of them were able to really have a go at their Vitamin C deficiencies.

Lara appeared at the other end of the café and I waved.

"How were the dolphins?"

She smiled. "They were really good."

"Jumping?"

"Oh yes. Many of them."

"Well, would you like something from the café or would you like to go in?"

"I think we should go in."

The exhibition was very impressive, with the words of participants, interactive displays and items found on the battlefield. The battle had been all over in an hour. The clansmen had been pounded by artillery, and when they had charged the redcoat lines, they had been cut down by musketfire. The Bonnie Prince was led from the field, leaving around 2,000 dead clansmen on the field, and about 50 of Cumberland's redcoats.

"What do you think?" I asked Lara. I was uncertain whether her English would be good enough to pick up some of the narrative.

"It was bad, I think. So many men died."

We walked out of the darkened visitor centre into the sunshine on the battle-field itself. Tussocky grass and heather covered the site, with woodland off to the sides.

"What do you do, Lara?"

"I am a teacher."

"Do you teach English? Your English is very good."

"No. History."

"Ah."

There was a lot of history here. We made our way to a large memorial. At least twice my height, it was built from large boulders and bore an inscription: 'The Battle of Culloden was fought on this moor, 16th April 1746. The graves of the gallant highlanders who fought for Scotland and Bonnie Prince Charlie are marked by the names of their clans.'

We found 'Clan Cameron' roughly inscribed on a stone where men had charged and died. Then 'Clan Donald', 'Clan Maclean' and more.

It was odd, standing in warm sunshine, chatting, where so many had been killed. It hadn't just been the battle that brought about the deaths. The government forces were brutal. Over the weeks and months following Culloden, clansmen and their families were butchered and their cattle driven off. Clan leaders who had supported Charles were executed as traitors.

Carrying weapons was forbidden. Even the wearing of tartan and kilts was outlawed. Everything was done to bring down the clan system, with clan leaders, even those supporting the King, losing their hereditary rights over their people. The Clearances, a couple of generations on, would finish the task. A further couple of generations on again, Queen Victoria, along with Dukes of this and Earls of that would have new designs of tartan invented for them and a whole new legend of the clans would take off, pretty much unrelated to the real people of the glens and islands.

Even Bonnie Prince Charlie and Flora MacDonald would become figures of romance rather than traitors to the King.

"Do you think that's enough of Culloden?" I asked.

"I think so."

We walked back through the visitor centre to the car park.

"Scott," I said. "This is Lara. Lara, Scott."

Actually I didn't say that. There was a possibility that the meaning might get lost in translation.

We walked on down through lanes in the sun, past stone walls and small fields. Beyond a gurgling river we came to a sign for 'Clava Cairns'. I left Scott in the car park, where a single car was parked in the warmth of the afternoon, its owners at the far end of the field amongst what looked disappointingly like piles of stones set amongst trees.

It was only as we got closer that the four large piles became more than that. It was as if rings of boulders, each probably thirty metres across, had been entirely filled with large, rounded stones up to waist height, just leaving a path through to the centre for a single person to walk. In the middle of each was an empty area, the floor flat, the walls again of larger boulders and completely round. It was all very mysterious and atmospheric.

We took it in turns to walk in to the first of the cairns, puzzling what they might be, then returned to read the signs. The cairns had originally been higher and roofed over. The paths had been exactly aligned with the midwinter solstice sun, so that it would shine on a quartz stone at the very back of the pathway. Perhaps they had been graves for bronze-age man. Or perhaps they had been the cathedrals of the time.

The owners of the car had gone and we had the field to ourselves to mooch into all four of the cairns, the sun glinting through the leaves of trees swaying in the breeze. I checked the time. It was mid-afternoon, and I had hills to cycle before I reached Tomatin.

"I'm afraid I have to carry on," I said.

"Of course. Yes, you go."

"What will you do? When is your bus back to Inverness?"

"Not for a while yet, but I will be happy here. I have my sketch pad."

I looked around. Yes, it would be a good place to sit and sketch, absolutely peaceful as leaves rustled and birds sang in the trees around the stones.

"Oh, fine. Well -"

We were interrupted by the sound of a coach turning into the car park. We watched as it disgorged men in golf shirts and women in sensible trousers, loud voices drifting towards us above the sound of the engine.

"I don't believe this," Lara said.

"What?"

"They are German. It is a German bus."

I stifled a grin. "Ah."

"And listen, the driver is not even switching off the motor."

It was true, the sound of diesel fumes pumping into the quiet air of Clava Cairns continued as the noise of loud German voices approached.

I glanced at my watch.

"You have to go."

"I'm afraid I do. Will you stay?"

"I will sit over there under a tree with my sketch book and wait until they have gone. I don't think they will be here long."

"Well then, this is goodbye."

She leaned forward and gave me a combined German handshake and kiss on the cheek. "It was very good to meet you," she said.

"And you. Send me a text to tell me you have got back to Inverness safely."

"I will. And you must be very careful on your bike."

"I will."

As I walked back to Scott, avoiding massed Germans, Lara was already making herself comfortable in the shade of a tree.

The road ran alongside the field and Lara waved as we set off.

For half a mile the road ran along the bottom of the valley, a warm sheltered ride, absolutely flat. Then there was a right-angle turn and suddenly I was climbing steep, steep up.

There was a possibility that I had reached the edge of the Cairngorms.

Legs burning, face red with heat and exertion, lungs bursting for air, I came to another right-angle turn. I stopped, gazing breathlessly across to Culloden Moor and down to Clava Cairns by the stream and the woodland below. I wondered if the coach had moved on, and peace returned.

When I restarted, I was pedalling along the face of the ridge, a minor road which rose and fell gradually. A railway line appeared and it occurred to me that this had been my route north by train. Niall and I had probably been preparing to change trains at Inverness just here.

Then we were falling, back into the valley, and ahead and below was the A9, cars and lorries streaming north and south, the 21st century intruding on the quietness of the ancient hills.

Just before reaching the A9, we came to a junction. The little blue cycle route signs took me off left, on a wide but quiet road, presumably the main road before the modern road was built. It even had a white line down the middle. The new road disappeared from sight on a wider loop southwards, and we climbed a long hill, suddenly coming into real mountains.

On either side the land changed to heather and tussocky grasses, with yellow broom adding colour to the sun-lit green of the landscape. A skylark rose chirruping into the air, flying up and away out of view, its distant song still carrying down to me. There was a beauty here, and a freshness of air. I could see why some new and very smart houses had been built along the roadside, an easy commute into Inverness.

The road rose and fell amongst forestry plantations. The railway line came in to join the road. Then the A9 reappeared and we scooted along parallel to the busy trunk road, passing a loch, dark blue in the sunshine, and with high mountains starting to gather on either side. My map told me that the summit on the right was Carn n h-Easgainn and the one on the left Meall a' Bhreacraibh. Marvelous names which I didn't have the first clue how to pronounce.

The old road ended, covered over by the new, and the route became a cycle lane close by the new road. The traffic noise should have been overwhelming, but somehow my brain cut out the distraction, concentrating on steering between encroaching pink and yellow lupins, purple heathers, and yellow broom. When the undergrowth did recede back to the edges of the path, the mountains came into focus, green, bare and brooding on each side.

I was past the sign for my bed-and-breakfast before I realised I had missed it and was heading towards Tomatin. I glanced at my watch. 4.45pm.

4.45pm!

"Scott," I said. "The distillery shop. Tomatin Distillery Shop.

They probably close at five."

"Yes, it would be truly awful to miss out on a distillery."

Feet hard down on the pedals, I sped towards Tomatin village.

Another sign: 'Tomatin Distillery'.

"Yes!"

4.55.

Up a well-made road.

Five o'clock.

"Aaagghhh!"

Past houses and distillery buildings.

5.02.

A sign: SHOP.

Three people were standing at the door of the building, one holding a key, as I bore down on them.

"Are you still open?"

A lady said, "No, I'm sorry. It's three minutes past five. We're just locking up."

"It's just, well, I'm cycling across Scotland, and I really wanted to get a miniature at each distillery."

"Oh. In that case…" She turned to her colleagues. "You go. I'll just open up again for this gentleman."

"But- " I stammered. "Thank you. That's wonderful of you."

I can report that the miniature bottle of the Tomatin Single Highland Malt Scotch Whisky, Aged 12 Years, comes in a small black and gold tube; that the distillery was Established in 1897; that the contents were Distilled with Pride; that the tube and bottle somehow managed to remain intact until after their new owner returned home; and that it tasted powerfully good. (Michael Jackson is more precise. He says the 12-year-old malt has a Nose of '*biscuity sweetness*', a Body that is '*sweet and velvety*', a Palate that is '*mellow and round, toffeeish, soft spices, pine nuts*', and a Finish that is '*sweet with a pleasant refreshing mintiness*'. I am in no position to disagree, and could probably spend a long time working out that he was right all along.)

I am also open to sponsorship offers. I am perfectly prepared to cycle with Tomatin across my back, though I do draw the line at 'Aged 12 Years'.

After many "Thank you"s I let the lady lock up again, and drifted back down the hill, at the bottom spotting another sign, this time for the Tomatin Inn. I dug out my phone and tried to ring the bed-and-breakfast to tell them that I would eat first and then come along. The number wasn't getting through. I tried again and failed, and so set off for the Inn.

I found myself eating scampi and chips in front of the Inn's television watching a news report of a former prisoner-of-war at the Italian Chapel in Orkney returning there from Italy. It felt a little disorientating, days after reading the visitors book. Was it another former prisoner? Surely not. Just news delayed for a quiet day? Probably.

My phone rang. A woman's voice, announcing the name of the bed-and-breakfast. Quite loudly, I thought.

"Oh, hi, yes," I said. "I tried to call you. I'm at the Tomatin Inn. I thought I would eat first then come back and find you."

Silence.

"Hello?"

"Eat first?"

"Yes. Is that OK?"

"It would be, except that you booked a meal here."

There was ice in her voice.

"Ah. Oh. Sorry. Did I?"

"Yes."

"Oh. Sorry."

She sighed. Long and meaningfully. "I suppose I can eat it myself tomorrow night."

"Right. Well, good. Thank you."

I didn't rush to get to the bed-and-breakfast, but before long I had no choice, and I said sorry all over again, standing on the doorstep.

"I could charge you for it," she said, holding the door open and blocking the entrance at the same time. An excellent example of multi-tasking which I can only aspire to.

"Yes, do that."

"No, I won't." She looked me up and down. "But I could."

"Right."

She stood back and her eyes fixed on my trainers. I reached down and took them off.

"This way."

She led me upstairs and showed me a room. Single bed. TV. Shower room. Small but clean. Functional.

"Don't open the window when the light goes. The midges will swarm in."

"No."

I followed her back downstairs, and she watched as I removed the panniers from Scott. As I stood there holding the panniers, she reached forward and grasped his handle-bars.

"I will put your bike round the back. I have," she said, "German Shepherds."

I could swear Scott trembled as I let him be led away.

Captain's log: Day Eight

Target:	21.0 miles	33.6 Km
Actual distance:	24.6 miles	39.4 Km
Average speed:	9.5 mph	15.2 Kmph
Maximum speed:	27.5 mph	44.0 Kmph
Total distance:	304.7 miles	487.5 Km

I tried really hard not to do anything else wrong.

I stood my coffee mug down carefully on a mat.

I kept the window firmly closed.

And I worried about Scott. A little.

I read till late, about 11.30, the house absolutely quiet.

When I went through to the loo, my elbow caught my wash-bag. I grabbed for it as it fell from the shelf. That deflected it against the sink. There it exploded into its constituent parts. Razor, shower gel, toothpaste, toothbrush and shampoo flew in multiple directions, each hitting a really quite loud surface, before cascading on to the floor-tiles.

Outside, a German Shepherd barked.

Day Nine

**Target: 41 miles / 65.6 Km
From Tomatin to Newtonmore
via Carrbridge, Boat of Garten & Aviemore**

As I entered the breakfast room, a couple at the far end left. There was nobody else at all. No music. No radio. No traffic noise. Just a tock, tock, tock from a grandfather clock.

I sat at a small table laid with starched white linen and set for breakfast, and I waited.

I waited some more, consciously stopping my fingers drumming on the table.

It began to dawn on me that she might not even know I was downstairs. It felt unwise to call out, or walk through to the kitchen.

There was no bell. And to be honest, even if there had been one, I wouldn't have rung it.

I put my head around the hall door. Nobody.

Plan B, I thought.

I crept back upstairs, gently re-opened my bedroom door, took a deep breath, and slammed it. Then I clumped down the stairs. Halfway down, I realised that she was waiting at the bottom, watching me, and there was maybe a hesitation in my step from there on. I was just a little uncertain whether she had seen the whole episode.

"Morning," I said cheerily.

Slight pause. "Breakfast?"

It's possible I was a little over-anxious by now, but my imagination took hold and I had visions of last night's meat and two veg; custard and spotted dick.

"Please."

Would it be re-warmed, or would the custard form a thick, congealed skin over the suet pudding? I remembered my mum making us spotted dick on a Saturday lunch time, just before I set off for football, probably following steak-and-kidney pudding, and saying, "It'll give you ballast."

What my host actually brought was bacon, eggs and the works. It was very nice, and there was the semblance of a smile. It occurred to me that I might have misjudged the situation.

I smiled back.

"Thank you," I said. "Um, lovely breakfast. And, er, nice room. Thanks."

"You're welcome," she said. "I hope you have a good ride today."

Yes, slight misjudgement there.

Scott was already by the front door when I made my way out.

"How were the German Shepherds, Scott?"

"They barked. Something disturbed them."

"Oh?"

"Yes."

"Shame."

I loaded the panniers on to Scott. The sight-seeing was over for a few days. Today was going to be a hard day. I wouldn't mention it just yet.

The climb to Slochd Summit started about ten minutes after leaving the bed-and-breakfast. Slochd Summit would be the second highest point on my ride.

"Just around the next bend, Scott."

We were on the old A-road again, wide with just the odd car humming past, and running parallel to the railway and the A9. I worked to block out the noise of the lorries just a short distance away across the valley.

The climb was mostly not too steep but a bit relentless, so I had time to take in my surroundings. From a distance the land was either the dark green of forestry or the mid-green of long tussocky grass. But closer to, along either side of the road, the green was interspersed with the colours of wild flowers – noon-day-sun buttercups (I think they were buttercups), heather in purple or pink plumage, and then – my botanical knowledge now wholly exhausted – the white cotton-topped plants I had seen up on the north coast. Oh and some pink flowers with thin petals; they were pretty.

As we climbed, the forestry disappeared and the route headed up into a gap between the mountains. The road ducked under the railway, and when it emerged, I was standing on the edge of the A9, the lorries thundering past. The old A-road had gone, and in its place was a cycle lane next to the main road. The familiar blue cycle-route sign had an addition: 'Risk of ice in winter'. I could believe it.

The cycle lane was excellent for a slow-but-steady cyclist with a Scott-of-a-bike, and in spite of my closeness to the main road, I enjoyed the gathering wildness of the mountains. Rock and stone were emerging more and more from tangles of heather on the hillsides above. The odd dip and then longer climb took me ever higher. Pot-holes and cracks in the cycle-lane were growing and the shrubbery was getting long on each side, but there was no risk – I was going too slowly to come off in a pot-hole.

At a gate, the old road re-emerged as a spur off the A9. I negotiated the gate with two hands while holding up a top-heavy bicycle with my other hand. I glanced up to the main road and four cyclists were flying past in line, heads down, lycra-covered thighs pumping.

As they vanished behind a line of trees, a shout drifted across from them.

"Stoppp!"

The four reappeared, drifting down the slope to where I had managed to close the gate without actually falling over. Something of a triumph really, I thought.

"Is that a cycle track?" one asked.

I cast an eye over the four of them, the clothing lyrcra'd to their frames, the long leg muscles that bespoke long-distance cyclists, the thin-framed, drop-handled, road bikes with tiny packs tucked behind pencil-thin saddles.

"Well, yes," I said, "and it's a really nice bike route, but it does have the odd pot hole, and it's a bit overgrown."

"Ah. Not quick then."

I showed them the route on my map. "It suits us. Me. But, well…"

They looked at each other.

"Stick to the main road then?"

One of them pulled a face. "If we have to," he said.

"How far are you going tonight?" I asked. "Carbisdale Castle is good."

"We're not stopping till John O'Groats."

I was stunned.

"John O'Groats? But that's… well… that's a really long way. How far are you going each day?"

"150 miles."

"Wow."

"The rest of us would be happy with 100 miles, but he," he nodded at one of his chums, "goes in front and doesn't stop."

"So where have you come from?"

"We started at Chelmsford, cycled to Land's End, then up to here. We'll stay at John O'Groats tonight, then head off back to Chelmsford."

They wouldn't, I thought, be stopping to look at castles, or dolphins, or even the view too often. But they were good guys, laughing and poking each other. There was a real camaraderie.

"Quick pee," one said.

They all leaned their bikes against the gate and headed to the bushes, backs to me, four in row, joking and giggling.

I got back in the saddle, and checked my map.

"Right then, we'll be off," one said, and they mounted up, clicking bike-shoes into pedals. "See you now. Take care."

And they were gone, joining the fast-moving traffic, wheel to wheel, one slip-streaming another.

"Scott," I said. "From now on we will be a single lean-mean-cycling-machine."

We set off fast, picking up speed, really pretty quick.

Unfortunately the down-hill slope only lasted a few metres.

I changed gear as we hit an up-hill slope. And then again. And then again.

Scott said, "How's the old lean-mean-cycling-machine going?"

I stopped, leaning forward on the handle-bars.

"Not as well as it could," I said. "If we're honest."

Another mile of up, and there was a sign.

SLOCHD SUMMIT
1328 ft (405 m)
ABOVE SEA LEVEL

I took a photo of myself, and when I looked at it, realised that I did seem a bit slochd, a slightly lop-sided smile and wrinkles under my eyes, topped off with my bike helmet at a funny angle. Definitely slochd, I thought.

Even so, I had made it to one of the highest points on the route and that felt like something of an achievement, cycling the ups and downs from sea level at Inverness the day before. It should mean a down-hill stretch into the heart of the Cairngorms, then another uphill to Drumochter Summit – higher again. There was still a long way to go to the border.

The route did begin to drop, the old road still shadowing the new road and the railway, swinging and twisting around the hillside with more trees appearing and the land less rugged and bony.

Civilisation appeared. A house set amongst trees in a dip in the road, with two black chicken-y looking birds strutting across the road. I remembered a book I had taken from my bookshelves before I had left, 'The Complete Book of British Birds'. I had scanned through for Scottish birds to look out for on my journey and there had been a picture of a black chicken-y looking bird, the elusive bird of the Scottish highlands – the capercaillie, 'turkey-sized giants of the forest'.

'A quiet observer,' the book had said, 'may be lucky enough to see one crash out of a tree'. Well, here I was, slowing and stopping, marvelling at seeing two such rare birds, strutting and clucking across the road by a small farm. 'Many people,' the book went on, 'have been attacked by raging capercaillies.'

It was true that these two had not crashed out of trees. Nor were they particularly raging. In fact, now that I studied them, they did seem a little more chicken-sized than turkey-sized.

In fact, perhaps they were black grouse: 'males raise their lyre-shaped tails, inflate their blue necks and make a bubbling dove-like cooing', says The Complete Book.

One of them stared directly at me and clucked, a bit, well, chicken-like.

"Have you ever wondered," Scott said, "if you might be ornithologically challenged?"

I ignored him. I knew what I had seen.

The road dropped again into Carrbridge, where a tree trunk had been carved into a tree-trunk-sized head complete with flowing beard and droopy moustache. The head had then been placed a little incongruously next to a little triangular flower bed set into a lawn. It was impressive though, no doubt a product of the 'Carve Carrbridge' competition, which I gathered attracted chainsaw-carvers from far and wide. Mind you, Carrbridge's 'World Porridge Championship' probably also attracted porridge-makers from far and wide. I probably wouldn't win either, my talents with a chainsaw so far untried and my porridge-making skills only likely to be rewarded if there was a special prize for lumps. In fact, the chainsaw might come in very handy for dealing with my porridge.

Carrbridge was actually more famous for its bridge than for its porridge or wood-carving – at least outside the competitive worlds of porridge-making and wood-carving.

There were two bridges. The one I stood on carried a road and allowed a view towards the other – a single unsupported arch of narrow grey stones sandwiched against each other, and clearly defying gravity. The bridge seemed to throw itself upwards from a rock-shelf on one side of the gushing river towards the other side, losing momentum but just clinging on to the rock shelf on the far side.

It made a fantastic picture; within the frame of the bridge, white water rushed over rocks and tumbled into a deep trough, where it became a peaty-brown surge of power. The bridge above looked so fragile, barely able to carry its own weight let alone the weight of anyone crossing it. That made it all the more unlikely when two young men climbed over a fence and posed part way up the delicate arch, so that their female admirers could take photographs.

"Scott," I said. "Is it just me being grumpy or is that not a good idea?"

"It's you being grumpy *and* it's not a good idea."

"Fair enough."

A little shop just over the bridge had a sign outside advertising ice creams, and I decided that part of a cure for grumpiness could well be ice cream.

The first part of the ride on from Carrbridge to Boat of Garten (now there's an unusual name for a land-locked village) was pleasant, in and out of stands of conifers along a quiet road. When I joined the busy main road for a while, there was a cycle lane.

Boat of Garten was a surprise. It was a homely lowland place, with retirement bungalows and local shops. But when I lifted my eyes, the hazy distance showed a wall of mountains. Today, it was just a haze. But these were real mountains, the highest summits of the Cairngorms, and Boat of Garten didn't seem to fit somehow.

I had a mission in Boat of Garten. Tom, my neighbour, has a passion for railways, and I could under no circumstances go through Boat of Garten without visiting the Strathspey Steam Railway.

At the far end of the town, a sign pointed to the station by way of the Golf and Tennis Club car park. A woman in a pink-diamond sweater was lifting her clubs from the boot of her car, and I looked up at the mountains again, just to check where I was.

A rusting locomotive dominated one end of the station car park. The station itself was quiet, and perhaps wouldn't get busy with its tourist traffic to and from Aviemore until later in the day.

A man was standing by his car and climbing into oily blue overalls. Scott and I scrunched through the gravel to him.

"You look ready for work," I said.

"Oh, I'll just be tinkering," he said. "Anything they say needs tinkering with, I'll tinker with it."

"Do you live in the town?"

"No, I've driven up from Dundee."

"That's a good round-trip."

"Yes, it's getting harder for volunteers now. To come so often. With the petrol costs."

"I'm sure. But you still come though. I imagine…" I stopped, wondering how to put it. "I imagine you love it."

He had a sheepish grin. "Oh yes."

Four trains a day would steam their way up the Strathspey Railway, partly for the pleasure of tourists, but mostly, I thought, for the pleasure of my friend in his oily overalls and his fellow enthusiasts.

I found some parked steam trains and took a photo for Tom. Mission accomplished.

Just out of the town, the road led me over the River Spey. Speyside had more whisky distilleries than you could comfortably shake a stick at. I had seriously contemplated changing my route to give it a try, but in the end I had decided that there were only so many detours I could take. Mind you, it was another good excuse to come back.

I spotted a large bird circling high in the sky, and stopped to watch.

"Scott," I said. "Look. A golden eagle."

"A golden eagle."

"Yes."

"Is it golden?"

I squinted up into the sky. It was quite a long way away.

"Well. Hard to tell from here."

"And is it an eagle?"

I looked again. I was not entirely sure.

"Um."

"Still challenged, are we?"

When I was a lad, I was given 'I-Spy' books for long car journeys. You had to tick off things along the route as you spotted them.

Horse: tick.

Oak tree: tick.

Zebra crossing: tick.

I used to cheat. Well, not cheat exactly. But if there was something dubious, I would still tick. 'I think that was a donkey in that field'. 'It was a cow.' 'No, it was a donkey.'

Donkey: tick.

If you completed an I-Spy book, you could send it off to Big Chief I-Spy, who I seem to remember would send you a feather and a certificate. Even with cheating, I don't think I ever got that far.

Anyway, if I'd brought an 'I-Spy Nature' book for Scotland, it would now read:

Deer: tick

Dolphins: tick

Capercaillies: tick

Golden Eagle: tick

And I would keep a firm look out for grizzly bears.

My road followed the Spey, slicing through old birch woodland and new forestry, passing old cottages and new homes with double garages and large gardens. We were climbing and falling, drawing closer to the mountains.

At the top of rises and with the land clear of forest and houses, the view south and east was across scrubby heather and yellow-tipped broom towards peaks reaching up towards dark and ominous clouds. There was still snow on summits

137

and in gullies, not yet melted by July in Scotland. Not too far away, my map showed the Cairngorm Mountain Ski Centre, and beyond it Bynack More at 1,090m high. Bynack More was not alone. A whole mountain range stretched away into the distance, ridges in shades of grey and blue, broken by patches of white. These were the Cairngorms, with Ben Macdui, the Black Pig, amongst them, the second highest mountain in Scotland at well over 4,000 foot in old money and over 1,300 metres in decimal currency, and it is surrounded by other giants.

Tomorrow I would be climbing up through the mountains. Not as high, of course, but up over Drumochter Pass, the highest point in my journey. I would be sharing the pass with a rail line – the highest railway line in Britain, in fact. I would take a photo for Tom.

Something lizardy ran across the road and vanished into a ditch.

Something lizardy: tick.

A sharp turn and we were suddenly in civilisation. My map said, 'There are many excellent mountain bike routes in the Rothiemurchus Estate,' and I was prepared to believe it from the number of people suddenly around on bikes. There were families cycling on little bike lanes from holiday homes set back in amongst forest, and groups of muddy, exhausted men heading in the same direction as me, seemingly all following signs for Aviemore.

Aviemore was a shock. Just a few minutes earlier, I had been looking across to those vast dark mountains. Now I was cycling past a Hilton Hotel on the way into a main street lined with concrete-boxes of shops, their plate glass windows reflecting the multitudes of cars and coaches trying to find somewhere to park. There were the same high-street names to be found in Surbiton and Harrogate. It didn't feel at all right seeing a Tescos just here. But there it was; and there I was, buying a sandwich.

In my defence, I had cycled 22 miles with only an ice

cream to sustain me along the way. I was very hungry.

Set back from the main street were large and very expensive-looking hotels; one of them eight storeys high. I thought of little Carrbridge and Boat of Garten just back up the road. This just didn't seem right.

I left Scott in a car park and made my way along the street looking for somewhere to sit and eat. It wasn't easy. There were people everywhere, buying jackets or jumpers, books or camping supplies.

A coach went past, banana-yellow with red writing two foot high on the side:

WILD & SEXY HAGGIS ADVENTURES.

The mind boggled.

Beyond the dark entrance to a nightclub stood a little garden, tucked between the main road and the rail line set up on an embankment. There was a bit of grass, some bushes, a little pond, and a rock.

"Hello, Rock," I said.

I ate my sandwich sitting on the rock, and decided that I would find toilets and then escape. The wildness of the journey until now hadn't prepared me for Aviemore.

I negotiated my way back along the pavement, dodging the families and dog-walkers, the lycra-clad cyclists and heavy-booted hill-walkers. The station was a considerable contrast – cream-painted wood-panelling, dark red window frames, doors and ironwork. A restaurant occupied part of the building, and I slid between tables to reach the toilets, mulling over just how it was that an Australian-themed restaurant had seemed a good idea for one of the highest railway stations in Scotland.

'Mind the Kangaroo' sign: tick.

I found Scott again back at the car park.

"How was Aviemore?" he said.

"Wild, sexy and adventurous."

"You were only gone twenty minutes."

"I work fast."

From Aviemore southwards I had the option of using the old main road, which was now a B-road but looked from the map as though it comfortably avoided too many hills and was pretty well straight. It would be quiet; all the traffic would be running a few hundred metres away on the new main road. For some reason though, the Sustrans cycle route was on a different B-road on the east side of the Spey, one which appeared not to avoid the hills, and which crinkled and bent with the landscape. Sustrans, I reasoned, must have chosen that road for a reason.

We set off back past Rothiemurchus, and then on to what became a wonderful road. Looking west across the wide Spey valley, all was grassy and tame in a broken sunshine, with hedges and trees marking order and endeavour. But beyond the valley-bottom, blue shadows of mountains insisted that this was highland country, and eastwards those walls of mountains a few short miles away still reared up into the cloud.

Then the road rose and we were bucking and weaving through moorland and woodland. We passed the occasional large house, but each was easily swallowed back into the wilderness of tree and heather. Then a sharp turn and I was on a bridge over the most beautiful of waterfalls. There was not the deep fall of water as at Shin, but it was unexpected and glorious the way the river gushed and poured through and over hard grey blocks of stone, splitting and gouging a path for itself. Crannies in the rock on either side gave tiny footholds to silver birches, thin and stringy, the green of their leaves sharp against the pumice-grey stone that clutched at their roots. I leant Scott against the bridge and marvelled at the scene, letting the tumbling noise of rushing water rise past me, the air fresh and clean above a river which had risen in the heights above me – Sgòran Dubh Mór, Sgòr Gooith, Càrn Bàn Mór, Mullach Clach a Bhlàir. A different language, and a different place.

I pulled the map out. This was Feshiebridge.

Please don't visit it. It's mine.

My map also had some other information. About a mile away, it showed a large green teacup.

"Come on, Scott," I said. "Time to go."

The green tea cup sign on the map took me down a short sharp hill to the Loch Insh Watersports Centre. We zoomed down and into a busy car park behind the Centre, a large-ish building directly above a wide beach. Sailing boats, canoes and windsurfers lined the shore, and a handful were out on the water, the windsurfers skimming fast across the loch in the breeze. Inside, a restaurant and bar were doing good trade and there was a gentle dispute going on between males and females. The television had two options – tennis from Wimbledon or Formula One. It wasn't a prolonged dispute; the men had control of the TV remote. Twas ever thus.

I sat on the balcony in the sun with my tea and watched the windsurfers. Unless I was mistaken, their wind was coming from the north, and that was very good news.

It was a stiff little climb back up to the road from the car park, but my legs did seem to be getting stronger with all this cycling through the highlands. I was on Day Nine, so maybe it was about time.

The road continued its twitching left and right, but was mostly flatter now, on the floor of the Spey valley, as we headed for the little town of Kingussie and beyond that my target for the day, Newtonmore. The wind was behind me and the sun in front. It wasn't a bad combination.

A sweeping turn and there in the distance was a giant ruin of a building on a grassy mound, its silhouette black against the blues and greens of distant mountains and closer valley. Ruthven Barracks dominated the green valley around it. If its builders wanted to control this most important route through the highlands, they had found the perfect place to do it.

It was built by a British government to try to control the highland clans who had rebelled in 1715. When Bonnie Prince Charlie led his own rebellion in 1745, the Barracks at first held out against attack, but the following year it was finally taken by the clans.

After the battle of Culloden, it was the rendezvous for around 3,000 of the defeated Jacobites. These were men intending to fight on, until a message arrived from the Prince that it was every man for himself. From the march into England, the retreat into the highlands, the bloody defeat at Culloden, and now this message, it must have been devastating. As they left, the Jacobites set fire to the Barracks, dispersing, and trying to escape before the redcoats could find them and take their revenge on them as rebels against the King. Those who were captured could expect – and would get – no mercy. Nor would many families and bystanders caught up in the aftermath. The King's son in charge of the round-up had the nickname of 'Butcher' Cumberland, and it was a deserved name. Those who burned the rugged, stone building here must have been desperate men, watching the flames and smoke curl up into the sky as they trudged hopelessly up into the hard mountains on either side.

I left Scott at the foot of the high mound, and made my way up to the ruins. Thick walls of stone blocks formed the barrack rooms and towers that surrounded the central courtyard. There were half a dozen people wandering around, poking into cellars or the roofless towers with their small empty windows.

A previous occupant of the site, the notorious 'Wolf of Badenoch' had his castle here in the fourteenth century. The ruthless 'Wolf' had plundered the highlands and destroyed Elgin Cathedral after having been excommunicated by the bishop. Here at Ruthven, he was said to have been visited one night by a dark stranger who challenged him to a game of chess. They played through the night, and by the following morning every other person in the castle was dead – the result of playing chess with the devil.

The stones that make up the ruins of Ruthven Barracks are probably the same stones that were in the walls of the Wolf's castle. I found it a sad place, in spite of a bright sun shining on waving grasses in the hay fields below.

The town of Kingussie was pretty, and I idled for a few minutes, considering the contrast to the Barracks and wondering how many of those who lived here now were descendants of clansfolk from the time of the Wolf and the Jacobites, brought to Kingussie and to the 'new town' up the road when the Clearances took their homes and land for sheep. The sheep have gone, and it is the mountains themselves that must provide the work – looking after the tourists, the walkers, bird-watchers, skiers, and even the cyclists.

I took the cycle route signs and they led on to a fabulous new tarmac'd cycleway through copses and fields, well away from the main road. Sharp right-angle turns took us over little bridges above sparkling streams. And there was wildlife. I had to stop dead as a duck and its duckling waddled across in front of me. It was an odd duck, with grey feathers at its throat and red eyes that watched me warily.

Red-eyed, grey-necked duck: tick

I was doing well at this.

The cycle-lane took me almost into Newtonmore. It was late in the afternoon after forty miles of cycling, but I felt good, and when a sign appeared for the Highland Folk

Museum, I noted that it was free, and decided on a quick charge round before it closed for the day. It was very good, especially the 'black houses' – reconstructions of 17th century homes, with shaggy thatched roofs sloping almost to ground level, with turf walls, and with heavy wood beams inside. This must have been how folk lived for centuries, peat burning in hearths, filling the roof and the lungs with smoke. The wealthier reconstructions had box beds and cupboards. Another had a weaver's loom. The poorer of the homes reminded me of the Iron Age reconstructions I had seen in Somerset, almost 2,000 years separating them, but very little else.

The cheery lady at the black houses was dressed in costume of the time – heavy woollen skirt, white apron and blouse, and walkie-talkie. It was a nice image, and I snook a photo, enjoying the incongruity, as my 17th century guide happily used a 21st century walkie-talkie to call up the 1950s bus that would take me to the 1930s farm and the 19th century school at the other end of the site. A young guy with a clipboard and a pen was observing the scene, and we exchanged a smile.

In the school, the teacher was tidying up for the day. She was another cheerful lady, but I gathered that school parties saw a stricter side to her. A strap, the Scots equivalent of the cane in England, was menacingly in view, though I am sure was unnecessary for the forceful lady in front of me.

"It's funny," she said, "but often the naughty children – and you can generally see exactly who it will be when they come in the door – are the ones who appreciate the strictness of a Victorian school. I asked one particularly difficult boy whether he preferred my strictness or how things are now. He thought about it, and said he would probably get on much better in a Victorian school."

The young chap with the clipboard came in, and I told them both my brother's story of the strap. We had been an English family living in Scotland, and my brother – so

144

family legend goes – had shouted out in class that the England rugby team would beat Scotland. Brought to the front for the strap, his young (Scottish) friend had shouted, "Take it like a man, Neil", and had also been given the strap.

"Things have changed," the schoolteacher said, smiling.

The young chap made a note on his clipboard.

The hostel was just up the road. It was an independent one, rather than part of the Scottish Youth Hostels Association. It had a large living/dining/kitchen area, with comfy armchairs, bookshelves and maps. There were clean dormitories and toilets, and a very good drying room for hanging washing. It was ideal.

There were to be just four of us that night, the owner told me through his beard. He showed me the shed where Scott would be spending the night, apparently next to the owner's bike.

"Are you cycling far?"

"To the border."

"That's good. Are you using the main road or the cycle route?"

"I avoid main roads at all costs. And the cycle lanes are really good."

"They're not too bad at the moment, but they're disintegrating. They've not used the right surface for up in the highlands. I've written to Sustrans, but of course it's too late now. The cycle lanes will be full of potholes before too long, and nobody's looking after it. It'll be no good for road bikes."

"It's OK for Scott."

"Scott?"

I indicated my fine figure of a bike.

"Ah. Scott."

"By the way, is there anywhere I can get some food?"

"There's a shop across the way."

So I bought a cardboardy looking ready-meal in the shop, and headed back to the hostel.

Young-man-with-clipboard was in the kitchen when I went back in, though, to be fair, he no longer held his clipboard.

"Hi," he said with an American accent.

"Hi, you're the man with the clipboard."

He smiled an embarrassed smile. "I'm doing my Masters at St Andrews University on ethics in museums which recreate history. I'm collecting data."

"Ah, so using the strap on children visiting the school might have ethical implications, do you think?"

"Well, I suppose, but that's not... Say, would you mind filling in a questionnaire?"

"OK. What about?"

"Well, it's better if you fill it in without me telling you what it's about. It might change the way you answer things. Oh, I'm Nick, by the way. I'm from Michigan."

"Mike."

There were thought-provoking questions. In a museum recreating a historical period, should age affect who took which roles? Well, 'yes'. What about gender? Ah, tricky. There wasn't a box for 'yes and no'. For a scene to look real, I thought, you had to take account of whether a male or a female would be doing a particular job. I put 'yes'. And then I read the next question and realised the first questions were softening me up.

In a museum recreating a historical period, should race affect who took which roles? So, I thought, in my young friend's America for example, a museum recreating slavery couldn't possibly have a black slave owner and a white slave. It would tell the wrong story about history. But that would have racial implications for employment. It would probably break the law, in fact. And that took me back to my answer on gender, and I thought maybe I was wrong on that one.

"Nick," I said, "I just don't know how to answer this."

"Difficult, isn't it?"

I ticked the box for 'Yes' on the race question. My pen hovered for a while, then I crossed it out, and ticked 'No'.

"And this is what your Masters is about?"

He grinned. "Yup."

I crossed out my tick for 'No' and re-ticked the 'Yes' box.

"Good luck," I said, and I handed him back the pen.

I microwaved my cardboardy meal, made a cup of tea for Nick and myself, and then a Dutch couple arrived and soon the kitchen was full of the smell of proper cooking. Lamb mince, herbs, tomatoes.

"I'm just going to wash my socks," I said.

Captain's log: Day Nine

Target:	41.0 miles	65.6 Km
Actual distance:	45.0 miles	72.0 Km
Average speed:	11.9 mph	19.0 Kmph
Maximum speed:	28.5 mph	45.6 Kmph
Total distance:	349.7 miles	559.5 Km

The Dutch pair went off to bed early. Nick and I stayed to chat. He was a serious young man, but a sense of humour poked through every now and then. He was going back to work in a museum in the USA when he had finished his Masters.

"Do you like it here?" I asked.

"Some yes, some no. I like the beer. And the whisky." He reached into a rucksack and pulled out a small silver hip-flask. "Try this. It's for taking up Ben Nevis when my friends come over."

"What is it?"

"Scotch," he said. "Ardbeg."

Ardbeg, from the island of Islay off the west coast – ('*Earthy, very peaty, smoky, salty, robust. A bedtime malt*').

I took a sip. It was delicious.

Ardbeg: Tick

Day Ten

Target: 42 miles / 67.2 Km
From Newtonmore to Pitlochry
via Dalwhinnie, Drumochter Pass and Blair Atholl

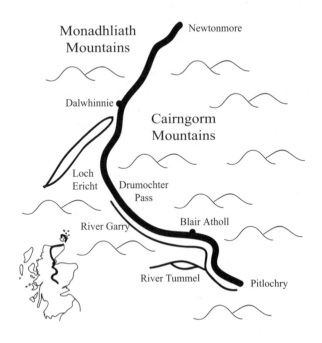

It was ten miles to Dalwhinnie along a quiet road that rose continuously, not steeply by any means, but most definitely continuously.

Dalwhinnie would be an important stop for me. Beyond there the next shelter and nourishment was twenty miles away, on the far side of the Drumochter Pass – the highest part of my journey. Interestingly, Dalwhinnie also had its own distillery (*'Lightly peaty. Cut grass and heather. Clear flavours against a very clean background. Aperitif'*). It would be the highest distillery on my journey. I wouldn't mention that to Scott.

There was just the odd farmhouse along the way as we climbed, leaving the Spey valley behind. To begin with, we were sandwiched between the railway line on one side and the A9 on the other. The rail line offered no trains to disturb the peace, but the A9 remained a constant source of noise. Again I found that somehow I could ignore the sound of the tankers, the lorries, the coaches and the cars. Perhaps it was the mountains closing in on either side. I relished their names. The small one must be Creag nam Bodach. That one Garbh-mheall Mór. The big one disappearing into the cloud would be Meall Chuaich. Real Tolkien-style names for some serious mountains.

The land was getting wilder, with the browny-green of out-of-season heather punctuated by the brighter greens of broom bushes and their vibrant yellow flowers. Clouds loomed ever darker over the mountains, threatening rain on the day I would cross Drumochter Pass. Still, a cup of tea, or something stronger, at Dalwhinnie Distillery's visitor centre, and that would give me a boost, even if the rain did come on.

Halfway to Dalwhinnie, the road took a different line to the A9 and the railway. We crossed to the far side of the Truim river and gradually drew away from my noisy partners. Strangely, I became more aware of the noise of the traffic as it receded. Like when the fridge in the kitchen stops vibrating, or the clock suddenly stops ticking, that's when you notice them.

As wild as the valley was at ground level, there was no getting past the stream of traffic, the train line, and the pylons, all alien to the wildness – the greens, the browns and the dark line of hills whose tops were now hidden by black clouds.

The copper hats of Dalwhinnie Distillery were visible from some way off, a burnished mirage in a heather desert. They drew slowly closer as I became aware that I was getting cold. The wind had got up, sliding down the valley towards me from the Pass somewhere in the distance. I zipped my coat up to my neck. It was probably too early for a dram of the hard stuff, but a cup of tea and taking away a miniature would be a good alternative.

Dalwhinnie Distillery was monochrome. The main building was a brilliant white, except for the black window frames. To the right were large, black, cylindrical vats elevated on black stilts above black tarmac. Silver hoops threaded their horizontal way around the cylinders. I leant Scott against a black lamppost on a pavement marked by white lines.

"Scott," I said, "we have cycled into a Laurel and Hardy film."

"Please don't do one of those intentional falling over things they do."

"Of course not."

It was not monochrome inside the visitor centre, and the inclination to try some slapstick comedy ebbed. Scott would be grateful when I told him.

The lighting was dim, the carpets were a muted tartan, and there was plenty of space for display boards on the history of Dalwhinnie Scotch whisky. What was slightly alarming though, was that there didn't seem to be a café. I was sure that my map had shown a big green teacup in Dalwhinnie and even a big green pint of beer.

A lady was standing behind a long counter which featured the various whisky-related options available.

"Um," I said. "Do you have a café?"

"I'm sorry, no."

"But…"

"There's a hotel down the road though."

What a relief. I did feel in need of succour before the last push up to Drumochter Pass. And if not succour, then possibly a cappuccino.

"In that case, can I just have a miniature?"

"Well, we don't really do miniatures. This is the smallest bottle we have."

She took out what appeared to be a half-size bottle of whisky. It was nicely displayed in a box, but considerably too big to fit into my panniers, and certainly too heavy to contemplate carrying for another few hundred miles.

I explained, and the lady graciously wished me well. I poked around the displays for a few minutes, long enough to discover that Dalwhinnie is the highest village in Scotland and that it has the coldest average temperature in Scotland.

I delivered the bad news to Scott about heights and temperatures, and then added the worst news. "My quest for whisky miniatures is not going as well as hoped."

"Don't tell me. You're going to need to come back."

"I'm going to need to come back."

We eased out of the car park, from black-and-white film to colour. Well, green, anyway.

"At least we got away without any hilarious slapstick incidents," he said.

"You have no sense of humour."

"No."

I looked him over, the tape-and-cable-tie arrangement holding the rear mudguard in place, the ridiculously over-padded saddle, and above all the name 'PURGATORY' printed on the side.

"Shame that."

The village of Dalwhinnie had a handful of houses and, fortunately, the hotel. I very much enjoyed the sign outside:

DALWHINNIE
TWINNED WITH LAS VEGAS

and it did cause my imagination to get the better of me.

It was possibly my giggling at the sign that caused me to misjudge my entry into the car park. I was going just a little too fast approaching the pavement outside the big plate-glass window of the restaurant. So it was that I had an audience at the window-table. I also had an audience in two of the cars in the car park, as families made ready to leave.

What my audience saw was my pulling the brakes a little too tightly, the back wheel sliding on a dried-up puddle, me slithering in slow-motion to the ground, Scott coming to rest gently on top of one leg, the other leg still firmly in its pedal-grip.

I seemed to be undamaged and in fact still in cycling position, though somehow now horizontally placed, rather than vertically.

Scott said, "I think the technical term is 'going arse over tip'."

"Some have a less genteel version of the phrase."

"Actually," he added, "I have to admit that slapstick does have something going for it."

"You're enjoying this just a bit too much."

"Oh yes," he said.

A concerned driver hopped out of his car and asked me if I was alright. I managed to pull my feet from their pedals and extricate myself from under Scott.

"Yes, yes, fine. Thank you. Fine."

Behind him in the cars, some faces were grinning.

I leaned Scott against a wall. "Dignity at all times," I said, and I went inside in search of a cappuccino.

An elderly couple were sitting at the table by the big window. They looked at me in a concerned, kindly way.

"I just thought I'd give you a bit of entertainment," I said.

It was a good place – a hotel, restaurant and café rolled into one. Not a lot like Las Vegas, to be honest, but modern, warm, with some pleasant background music and a good line in poached eggs on toast and cappuccino.

Feeling fortified for the final push over Drumochter Pass, I went back out to Scott. It was drizzling and cold. Not July weather, and I believed the lowest average temperature bit from the exhibition.

I was pulling on my waterproof jacket and zipping it up as two bikes pulled in, bearing large panniers and a fit-looking mid-thirties couple.

Neither of them went arse over tip in the car park.

They had ridden from Land's End to John O'Groats two years before and really enjoyed it. So now they were cycling between the opposite corners, Dover to Cape Wrath.

I recommended the poached eggs and the cappuccino.

A couple of miles south of Dalwhinnie, the new-ish cycle lane reappeared. The guy at the hostel was right; it was no good for road bikes. Scott, though, might have been designed for it. Scott was once a mountain bike, and had front suspension plus big wide tyres. The track looped up and down, a bit loose and with the odd pothole, but this was fun. There were quite a few patches of wild flowers as well – pink, white and yellow splashes of colour alongside my wheels. I hardly noticed that we were still climbing, at least until I looked across to a large sign by the railway line off to one side:

DRUIMUACHDER PASS
1484 ft (452m)
HIGHEST POINT ON RAIL NETWORK

It was, presumably, the original Gaelic name for the pass. I took a photo for Tom.

I checked the map. There were two mountains on the right, The Boar of Badenoch and The Sow of Atholl, and it was odd that Ben Macdui was also The Black Pig. There was definitely a piggy theme going on here. I took to speculating at the translation of A'Bhuideanach Bheag high up on my left. The Piglet of Cairngorm would have a ring to it, I thought.

That reminded me; Ben Macdui was reputed to be home to a Scots version of the yeti, Ferlas Mor – the Great Grey Man, who was either 10 foot tall or 30 foot, depending on who was telling the story of being chased off the mountains. I imagined my I-Spy book –

Ferlas Mor: __

I checked all around. Nothing obvious.

Mind you, I was grey. I was a man. Well, two out of three.

Ferlas Mor: tick

A little further on, the cycle lane rose to meet the main road with its charging traffic. The motorists had their own sign:

DRUMOCHTER SUMMIT
1516 feet (462 metres)
above sea level

I typed out a text and sent it off to friends and relatives: *'Have reached highest point on my route. Intend to free-wheel all the way to the border.'*

My brother Andy responded: *'Isn't there something called the Southern Uplands in the way?'*

'Probably a typing error.'

I realised that I was warm. The sun had come out. The wind had shifted and was behind me. And it was downhill all the way to the border.

Probably.

I managed to freewheel for about a hundred metres before the cycle lane began its rolling gait again. Even so, we were dropping now, the down hills longer than the ups. It was a shame to be stuck in the same valley as the busy road and railway line, electricity pylons and telephone lines, but still the mountains on either side somehow absorbed or deflected the 21st century. There was a long view to the right down Loch Garry, with the steep slopes of Meallan Buidhe and Meall na Leitreach reaching down to the water. There was Meall Brac and Glas Mheall Mòr, heather and scree-covered, rising to a sky with patches of blue. Their names rolled around my head, wonderful sounds.

Now, though, we were starting a long fall out of the highlands; we had crossed the watershed. North of the pass, the Spey was emptying in to the sea at a north-facing coast. Here I was in Glen Garry, and the river Garry would join the river Tummel, which would run into the Tay and find the sea on the east coast via Perth and Dundee. Tonight, at Pitlochry, would be my last night in the highlands, and I was sorry about that, even though I had significant places to look forward to. Stirling, the Kingdom of Fife, Edinburgh and of course those Southern Uplands.

The cycle lane ran out and we joined the old road again, making its quiet and leisurely way down the valley, as the heavy traffic took the A9. Woodland had begun to appear, and I pulled in for a drink and a biscuit where the river came close and I could see a tumbling waterfall through the trees. It was a gorgeous spot. All around me, white daisies and pink clover studded the long grass with colour, and silver birches fought to keep a purchase in the thin soil near the water. I sat on the edge of the river as it rounded and smoothed the layered grey rock, falling over small precipices into dark basins of water, bubbles frothing Guinness-like to the surface.

I pottered through the trees, feeling the bark of the silver birches, the grey lichen skrinkling under the hand, till I came across a memorial plaque set into a lone tree deep in the woodland. It was a heart-felt poem to a John Fyfe Fyvie, here in this beautiful scene, 'more of a friend than a brother'. It was hard to think of a better place for memories. The rain that had threatened earlier finally started as I read, dripping through the leaves, spattering my shirt, and I walked thoughtfully back to Scott.

With the rain getting heavier, I pulled my jacket, waterproof trousers and over-shoes from the panniers.

"Time to go, Scott," I said.

The rain was a blanket as I pedalled on, running down the road and spurting from under Scott's tyres. When the road ducked through a bridge underneath the A9, I looked at the bike computer and saw that I had ridden 30 miles that day. A good reason to stop, I thought. That and the lack of rain under the bridge.

After ten minutes, there was no sign of the rain easing, and I was getting chilly underneath the concrete canopy of the bridge. I checked the map. It was just another three miles to Blair Castle, former home to the Dukes of Atholl, open to Joe Public, and no doubt possessing a warm café.

We set off into the rain again and almost immediately came upon the House of Bruar. I had forgotten it was on the route – an upmarket emporium for clothing, gadgets, art and considerably more expensive food than I would be consuming on this trip. I turned off into the car park and mulled over finding a café inside where I could dry off. But it felt wrong somehow to be going into somewhere so utterly different to the land I had been cycling through. The modern buildings and the car park seemed to have no link to the country around. I looked up at the clouds. It was very black above me. I circled the car park. No, I thought, I will be strong. And damp.

Another couple of miles took me into the village of Blair Atholl, with signs for Blair Castle. As I pedalled up a long drive lined with tall trees, the rain eased, and was suddenly gone. I found myself in front of the castle. No stone ruin, this was a white-washed building of towers and coned turrets, with windows set in walls that must surely once have had just arrow-slits. It looked what it was – a real castle, hundreds of years old, that had been built on and converted by generations of owners.

I attached Scott to a fence, peeled off my waterproof trousers and over-shoes and hung them from his crossbar.

"Stay," I said.

The entrance hall was two storeys high and its wood panels held floor-to-ceiling displays of guns, swords, knives, shields and every other form of historical weapon you can think of.

"It's quite something," I said to a guide.

"The hall was built after the rest of the building to house these weapons."

"Specifically to do that?"

"Yes."

Hm.

Blair Castle was far from homely, but then it isn't a home any more. When the last Duke of Atholl died with no children, he left Blair Castle to a trust. The new Duke is South African and doesn't own the property, though apparently he comes here to inspect the Atholl Highlanders. Not a part of the British Army, they were officially sanctioned by Queen Victoria and are the only legal privately-owned army in Europe.

The castle's rooms reflected different periods of its history. There was the 16th century bedroom with its vaulted low ceiling, the 18th century dining room with its white stucco plaster walls, chandeliers and mahogany dining table, and the enormous 19th century ballroom with its high wood-beamed roof and row upon row of antlers on the walls.

The castle was besieged by Cromwell and also played a part in Bonnie Prince Charlie's war of 1745. The Earl held out for the King, while his eldest son was in command of the army for Charlie, the Young Pretender, and even besieged Blair Castle itself.

Finally, the tour led me to the café, surprisingly 21st century, warm and with a good supply of hot chocolate. It occurred to me that it must be days since I had even enquired about lemon drizzle cake in a café. I had almost given up my body to Vitamin C deficiency. This was serious.

"Excuse me, do you have lemon drizzle cake?"

"No, I'm sorry."

"Carrot cake?"

Yes. Carrot cake.

"Can I have a large slice please? It's for the Vitamin B."

By the time I had emerged, the castle was a brilliant white in the afternoon sunshine.

We were definitely on a downward trek now, and the cycling was easy and pleasant in the warmest part of the day. The roads were steaming dry and the tourists emerging after the downpour.

In Killiecrankie (no doubt the third of the Crankie brothers) I pulled into the visitor centre for the Soldier's Leap. I set off down a well-worn path through oak woods to see where a soldier had apparently jumped 18 foot across a gorge to escape Jacobite clansmen. It was all very well, but was it true? And I preferred my chanced-upon waterfalls to these with their gravel paths and signposts and fences.

By the waterfall, I glanced at my watch and found that the time was getting on for five o'clock. Pitlochry was five miles away and Pitlochry had two distilleries – Blair Athol (*'Redolent of shortbread and ginger cake. Spicy, nutty. A mid-afternoon malt?'*) and Edradour (*'Spicy. Minty. Creamy. After dinner'*). It would be mostly downhill and my legs, for some reason, had a new energy.

We zoomed past pretty woods, powered past river views, and scared the pants off a Japanese tourist with a camera standing in the road taking a photo of river views and pretty woods. Even so, it was after five when we hit downtown Pitlochry. We turned into Blair Athol Distillery (with a different spelling to Blair Atholl village) and I abandoned Scott to make it to the shop door. Which was shut. It was closed. I had missed another miniature.

We followed signs across a footbridge over the widening river to the theatre and the salmon ladder. What I really wanted was to see salmon leaping up a ladder, which was pretty clever of them. The ladder turned out to be more of a long set of linked concrete ponds, through which a salmon or trout could swim up past the high dam. I leaned over the wall to look down into the ponds, but they were so dark I could see nothing at all.

"Have you seen anything?" I asked an elderly couple leaning over the same wall.

"Not here. It's a bit early for them. You might try over there though," the man said, and he gestured towards a little hut.

I wandered across, to find a lady with a key waiting for a family to come out before she locked up for the day. Leaning past her, I could see a big glass tank, in front of which the family were ooh-ing, ah-ing and pointing.

"Do you mind if I…?"

"Go on then," the lady said.

As my eyes became accustomed to the darkness, the shape of a large salmon emerged through the glass. A tail flicked and a fishy head came close to the glass, its eye looking out incredulously at us.

It was big. In fact, in true angler style, I can assure you

that it was THIS big. No, no. **THIS** big.

Another flick and it was gone.

"Is the tank part of the fish-ladder then?" I asked.

"Yes, it is."

About 5,000 Atlantic salmon are counted in through here every year, finding their way back to their spawning grounds higher up in the streams that feed the rivers and lochs here.

It felt daft really, but it seemed a bit of a privilege to be so close to this king of fish on its 6,000 mile journey from the ocean. Quite, quite extraordinary.

Atlantic Salmon: tick.

Feeling hungry, (perhaps it was the salmon), I cycled back through the town and up the hill to the youth hostel. From the front garden of the large Victorian-looking building, there were views across the rooftops to the mountains I'd been cycling through.

The hostel was bigger than it looked from the outside, with a lounge, a kitchen for visitors and even a kitchen and staff to produce breakfasts for guests in the morning. I signed up for a cooked breakfast, and that made me feel even hungrier.

I squeezed Scott into a bike shed already containing half a dozen bikes, all quite a bit more professional than him, picked a bed in a so-far empty dormitory, showered and walked into town. Now I was really, really hungry.

The shops along the main street were older buildings, some with cast-iron and glass canopies over the pavements. Hanging baskets of fuchsias and pansies were everywhere. It was totally different to Aviemore. More woolly cardigan than softshell jacket. It was possible that the Wild and Sexy Haggis Tours passed on through in search of a more vibrant nightlife a few miles up the road.

I scanned menus in windows. I was looking for a cheap price and an over-full plate. One offering stood out above all the others: the 'Robert the Bruce Burger', an enormous steak-burger and chips. There really was no choice.

Captain's log: Day Ten

Target:	42.0 miles	67.2 Km
Actual distance:	47.6 miles	76.2 Km
Average speed:	12.7 mph	20.3 Kmph
(the fastest so far; see? downhill all the way)		
Maximum speed:	30.5 mph	48.8 Kmph
Total distance:	397.3 miles	635.6 Km

The hostel became reasonably full. There were a few singletons like myself; there was a youth group with two cheery female leaders; and there were a dozen heavily built German cyclists of an age and consistency that suggested a certain amount of German beer and sausage had been an integral part of their training programme.

One of the singletons was making coffee in the kitchen at the same time as me. He was tall, curly-haired, with a winning smile. Also from Germany, Rolf was teaching climbing courses here locally. We chatted about the merits of various European countries he and I had visited, but it soon became clear that he had plans for the evening.

One of the cheery female youth-group leaders poked her head through the door, caught his eye and waved a bottle of wine. Rolf winked at me, and the winning smile was out of the door considerably before you could say 'Ever-closer European Union'.

Day Eleven

Target: 44 miles / 70.4 Km
From Pitlochry to Crieff via Dunkeld

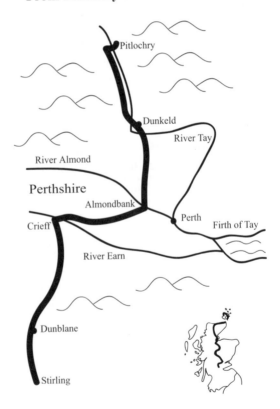

Today I would come out of the Highlands. Or at least I would if the lady behind the counter at the hostel could find the key to the bike shed. As things stood, I wasn't going anywhere. I had breakfasted amongst Germans with Lycra-covered paunches and raucous kids from the youth group. The lone female group leader had been having a little trouble quietening them. There had been no sign of her colleague, nor, coincidentally, of Rolf. Then I had gone out to extract Scott from the bike shed, but of course it had been locked.

"The key should be on the hook," the lady at the counter said.

She called a colleague and they searched the desk and the drawers, picked up keys and examined them, then put them back.

Her colleague said, "Is there a spare?"

"I really don't know."

I thought back to breakfast and the German group. "Have the German cyclists still got it, from when they got their bikes out?"

"Well, I hope not. They've already checked out. They may have gone."

I dashed through to the front of the hostel. There was a clicking as Teutonic cycling shoes slotted into pedals.

"Excuse me," I said. "Does anyone have the key to the bike shed? Die Schlüssel für das, um, Sched?"

There were some looks of non-understanding before one put a hand to his mouth.

"Ach. Die Schlüssel. Ja."

He pulled out a long key from a jacket pocket and handed it to me.

"Thanks," I said, with a certain amount of relief. "Danke. Danke schön!"

"Los," shouted the leader, and they were off down the steep hill into town. I imagined their momentum might be quite considerable by the time they reached the bottom of the hill.

Mind you, I expect they had good brakes. Vorsprung durch Technik, and all that.

I tried the key in the shed door and found that it worked.

"Scott, you're still here. I did wonder whether one of the Germans might have preferred you to their power-machines."

"You jest."

"Yes."

I returned the key to the lady at the desk, and she hung it carefully back on the hook. Then we were off down the hill into town, my own cooked-breakfast-inspired momentum not inconsiderable.

We were still on Cycle Route 7, though only for a while. Route 7 would be heading off west, upstream alongside the River Tay, then heading towards Glasgow and eventually right down to south-west Scotland. I was planning on riding further south before my own little jaunt westwards to Crieff and then tomorrow to Stirling. My route would be on country lanes and B-roads, this time on the opposite side of the valley to the A9.

The day was cool and dry, under a thin covering of high white cloud through which blue sky promised the occasional sun. Today should be a good day for cycling.

Route 7 signs took us over the same narrow suspension-bridge as the previous day. I was in less of a hurry though, and so stopped in the centre of the bridge to look up and down stream. The River Tummel was quite wide here, flooding out from the dam and its fish ladder. Dark hills lined the horizon, and closer to, the sun picked out a pub on the riverbank. Downstream, woods lined the banks, and the hills behind were lower and rounded. Tamed, almost.

A narrow lane took us up the side of the valley through woodland, only to drop down again for a view of the river rolling its way southwards. Climb and drop, climb and drop, it may not have been the easiest cycling, but it was gorgeous country, ending after five miles where the valley of the

Tummel joined the Tay valley coming in from the west. My route would be on the far side of the Tay, and Sustrans had used an old rail bridge to take the cycle route across, the railway lines having been replaced by wooden planks, some of which were a bit more ill-fitting and loose than was entirely comfortable.

On the far side, we joined a B-road. The blue-and-red Route 7 signs pointed west, and I was sad to see them go; they had been my guides since Inverness. It was true that I now had Route 77 signs, but only for a few miles. Then I would be on my own, and that might prove interesting.

We passed a posh-looking country house hotel, set in wide tree-speckled grounds, with tennis courts waiting patiently for players.

"Perhaps we should have stayed there, Scott?" I said.

"They probably have a dress code."

"Ah."

The road continued its ups and downs, winding through the edge of woodland, and then emerging for lovely views of the Tay as the river looped its way south along the valley floor. We emerged quite suddenly on to the A9, which was a little alarming until I realised that a cycle lane led alongside it. I allowed myself another little bout of alarm when the cycle lane crossed the Tay and heading back north again, but I kept faith with Sustrans and suddenly we dropped down to the river bank heading south for Dunkeld.

We were just yards from the flow of the river, drifting through trees, ferns and foxgloves, when a movement to my left caught my eye. A small deer, his eyes wide, more startled than me, was running alongside just two arm's lengths away, tan fur quivering as he leapt and scampered. I touched the brakes and the deer ran on, then peeled off into fern. A rustle of leaves and it was gone.

Deer Type 2: tick

A gentle downhill, and the river broadened as it rounded a bend, with a gravel beach shelving into the dark water. I stopped to take a photo and as I did, a bike carrying fully loaded front- and back-panniers came the other way. The rider was an older man, with greying hair on his helmetless head, and a tired-looking face.

"Hi," I said. "You look like you're going a long way."

He pulled to a halt by me. "I'm doing the Land's End to John O'Groats."

"That's great," I said, though from the way he said it, I was already sensing a lack of enthusiasm.

He said, "Well, I'm finding it really hard, to be honest."

"Oh dear, why's that?"

"It's rained every day. And I mean every day."

"You're by yourself?"

"Yes. And, well, I'm just finding it very tough. All the hills, you know."

He hadn't yet reached the Cairngorms. That didn't bode well.

"Where are you heading for today?"

"I've a bed-and-breakfast booked the other side of the Drumochter Pass. I can't say I'm looking forward to going over the Pass."

What was it my guide book had said: 'a relentless and exposed climb with no shelter or facilities whatsoever for 30Km'? It hadn't, in the end, felt like that for me, but I thought it might for my friend here.

"You'll be fine," I said, as brightly as I could. "You've come this far. You're now a lean, mean cycling machine."

He did smile. "I'm a tired, lean, mean cycling machine," he said, and he set himself to re-start.

A vision of Eeyore's long ears and droopy face came to me unbidden. "Hope it stays dry for you," I said.

"It won't."

He set off, and I watched him pushing slowly down on the pedals until he rounded a bend in the path on his way to the Drumochter Pass.

My track led into Dunkeld past the 'Parent Larch'. There

seemed to be various versions of the story of the Parent Larch, but the version I liked was that in the eighteenth century, five larches were brought into the country, with their seeds used by the Duke of Atholl to plant one and a half million trees around his estate, sometimes using a cannon to scatter the seeds. The Duke's scheme was pretty successful – this part of Perthshire is 'Big Tree Country', and it was true, there were some big trees, with this 'Parent Larch' the last of the five originals.

This all struck me as a tremendous way of gardening. ("Claire, I have a new planting scheme for the garden. Just stand clear of the cannon.")

Through the gate into the grounds of Dunkeld Abbey, the gentle slope of a tree-studded lawn fell away towards the Tay. The grass was speckled with daisies, the trees blending light and shade for benches facing the peaceful waters. From across the river came the muffled sound of drums, and through the trees were glimpses of what might have been a marching band. And then the silence returned, the river flowing on unruffled.

Half of the Abbey was a grey, solid, stone church, the other half an imposing ruin. I looked in on the ruins first, the high walls seemingly complete, with their thick buttresses and wide gothic and Norman arches stretching upwards. But there was no roof, and the floor was gone, replaced by grass and gravestones, a sad place really, just a reflection of former glory.

Inside the church was quite different though. There were people milling around taking in the high ceiling and the windows; there was real life here, even though the most impressive part of the church was a huge memorial tablet on the wall, complete with (I counted them) 33 brightly coloured coats of arms. There were shields for Atholl, Perth, Norfolk, Nottingham, Rothes and many more. Even Sinclair. Trust my ancestors to get a look in.

This had been a Christian site before the Christianity of

Rome became dominant. The Celtic church had come to Scotland from Ireland via the island of Iona on the west coast. When Viking raids made Iona unsafe in the 9th century, the relics of Iona's St Columba were brought to the monastery in Dunkeld. It would not have been a stone building; in fact it would probably have been indistinguishable from the huts I had seen at Newtonmore. This cathedral was built much later, and was burned to the ground twice. The small town had had an adventurous history before it had settled into National Trust for Scotland serenity.

A lane of white single-storey or two-storey houses, fronting straight on to the street, led down to the town square. On the corner stood the 'Ell House', a tall white building complete with another two coats of arms and an iron rod attached to the outside wall. An 'ell', I gathered from a sign, was the traditional measurement of length in Scotland until English 'yards' were made official in 1824. Before that, it was the 'ell', 37 inches long, with the exact measurement shown by the iron rod.

I was directed to toilets in a car park. It was a little stunning to find the toilets were manned (womanned really) and that there was a 30p charge. It was the sort of thing you would expect in France or at Euston Station, but not necessarily in Dunkeld. I paid up. Needs must. At least the toilets were smart and clean, with flowers in a vase. Considerably better than many an unmanned (or unwomanned) toilet in some other small towns along the way, so I supposed, reluctantly, there might be something to be said for it.

Then it was out along the road through adjoining Birnam, heading south. There was woodland on either side, and not just any wood. This was Birnam Wood, Shakespeare's Birnam Wood in 'Macbeth'.

Macbeth, according to the play, had murdered his King and assumed the throne, the witches telling him that:

Macbeth shall never vanquish'd be until
Great Birnam Wood to high Dunsinane Hill
Shall come against him.

So Macbeth was confident in his security until he was told:

As I did stand my watch upon the hill,
I looked toward Birnam and anon methought
The wood began to move.

Vengeful soldiers had plucked branches from the trees here to disguise their attack and Macbeth was doomed.

It was a good story, and some of it was true. There had been a real King Macbeth who had usurped the throne, and then himself been overthrown, though the Birnam Wood bit may have been artistic licence.

Through the other side of Birnam Wood, it became clear that we had left the highlands behind. We were in open country of grain fields punctuated by copses and trees. In Bankfoot, after 20 miles of cycling, I had intended another small stop, but there was nowhere to sit, so I found myself back on the bike again after a brief drink and biscuit. I was still following Route 77 signs, as the cycleway rolled towards Perth and from there to Dundee, altogether known as 'The Salmon Run'; pretty apt, given the salmon I had seen at Pitlochry, which must have passed Dundee and Perth on its way up the Tay and Tummel.

An idea occurred to me when I arrived in the village of Almondbank on 27 miles for the day, and not far short of the city of Perth. This was where I would be turning off Route 77 to find my own way to Crieff and then tomorrow down to Stirling and from there across to Fife. The weather was still dry, with just high cloud holding the sun at bay; I was feeling good (with most of today's cycling having been downhill or flat); and I would be at my bed-and-breakfast in Crieff by mid-afternoon. My idea was that I could maybe push straight on to Stirling that afternoon.

I bought a Scotch egg and a banana from a little shop

while I considered. I would certainly rather have time tomorrow morning in Stirling, to tour the castle perhaps, than time today at Crieff. It would make today a long cycling day, but would shorten what would have been a long day tomorrow.

I made my decision, phoned the Youth Hostel in Stirling to check they had space, and phoned the bed-and-breakfast in Crieff to apologetically say I would not be there that night.

There is a possibility that I had not worked out my mileage right as far as Stirling. There is also a possibility that my weather-reading skills were not finely honed. Another possibility is that I was over-estimating my fitness. At that stage, I was not aware of any of those three failings. If Scott knew, he was saying nothing.

I got lost cycling out of Almondbank.

I know. This was ridiculous. Almondbank was not exactly a vast metropolis and I was theoretically still on Route 77, just following the last of the familiar little signs until a turn-off that would take me through country lanes to Crieff. But I must have missed a Route 77 sign and instead followed a track under a canopy of trees alongside the little River Almond. It was only as I went further and further along the track, with there being no right turn and no more '77' signs, that I realised I must have gone wrong. I stopped to look at maps. I had the one very sensible one for Route 77, and one I had printed out from the internet of the back lanes to Crieff. It had travelled with me all this way, on ordinary paper, using ordinary ink, and was looking a bit disreputable. Actually, it was almost indecipherable.

A cyclist came up behind.

"Hi," I said. "I was looking for the road to Tibbermore."

"It's not this one."

"No."

He examined my indecipherable map, turning it this way and that, before handing it back dismissively.

"Just go on along here, turn right, right and left."

"Right. Right. Left."

"Right."

"Right. Thanks. Thanks very much."

We turned right, right and left and there was the main road, with a lane going off the other side to Tibbermore.

I actually had two indecipherable maps printed from the internet. The one showing the route to Crieff. The other from Crieff to Stirling. They made a dog-leg, and it did occur to me that if I had a slightly more sensible map, I could probably cycle direct to Stirling, saving a lot of mileage. As it was, I was committed to my route.

"Have I mentioned that you are an idiot?" Scott said.

"Yes."

Beyond hedges on either side of the lane, large wheat fields rolled off into the distance where low hills were covered with woodland. This was so very different compared with the highlands. It was hard to believe I had set off from Pitlochry just that morning, that Dalwhinnie and Aviemore and the Cairngorms were just beyond.

A sign appeared: 'Farm Shop and Restaurant'. It came as a surprise; there was barely any traffic on this quiet and restful country lane with no houses. Yet here, as the hedge ended, was a car park busy with cars, and a farm shop and restaurant notably busy with people.

There was a field entrance next to the car park. I laid Scott down and sat amongst tractor-squashed wheat stems to eat the Scotch egg and banana, glancing up occasionally at a darkening sky before pushing Scott around to the car park.

The restaurant was by no means small, but was very full. There was no table free at all, each and every one filled by the silver surfers of Perth having their afternoon teas. I felt positively young, even if the colour of my hair was not so different to theirs. I could ignore it. There were no mirrors. I was a lean, mean cycling machine.

My eyes lighted on a double-layer of shortbread biscuit topped with icing and a glace cherry, which my local baker calls a 'German Biscuit', and which I call 'Mum's shortbread biscuits with a glace cherry on top'. Here, it was an 'Empire Biscuit'.

I placed my order. An Empire biscuit and a large pot of tea. At least the Empire Biscuit had a glace cherry on top, which was almost certainly stuffed full of Vitamin C. And maybe B.

I retreated to a bench outside, where a waitress found me a few minutes later with a tray containing a pot of tea and an Empire Biscuit. She asked me my route, then said, "I'm planning on doing the Pitlochry Étape next year. It's 80 miles, but I've a year to train for it."

"Well, good luck."

She smiled. "Thanks. I might just need it."

I looked it up later, the Pitlochry Étape. I found that it was the only closed-road cycle challenge in Britain, open to all for a fee, and likely to attract about 3,000 cyclists for a hilly and beautiful course through the hills. It sounded fantastic.

My road onwards had long but extremely gentle rises and falls as it made its way towards Crieff through more fields of ripening grain, and then I was in the town of Crieff itself. I had had an expectation of somewhere posh, but there were just shops and houses much as any other small town, with teenagers larking around, pensioners with trolleys, and mothers with pushchairs. It seemed an OK sort of town, and I had been on the road for 54 miles already. Well more than my usual average.

There was even a distillery – the 'Famous Grouse Experience', with the blended Famous Grouse whisky on display at the little Glenturret Distillery. Good though The Famous Grouse is, I wasn't sure that I was quite up for an 'Experience'.

Even so, perhaps I ought to stay in Crieff. I tossed it around again, then thought, 'no, let's go for it'. I'd done a 70 mile day once on the trip. I could do it again. It would be good to push on to Stirling and have plenty of time there.

There was a Tourist Information Centre in Crieff and I was able to buy myself a proper map that would lead me almost to Stirling. It had some wonderful place names on it – Yetts o'Muckhart, Pool o'Muckhart and even Crook of Devon, which were a little out of place, unless one of the villains of Plymouth had decided to settle down in Perthshire.

We cycled out of Crieff on an A-road, but it was pretty quiet as far as the village of Muthill, where there were various scarecrows sticking out of windows, emerging from hedges and hanging from windows. Someone definitely had a sense of humour.

I had a choice now. I could turn off right on to a country lane, which would be pretty well free of traffic, but which went straight up a long fairly steep hill, or I could go on the A-road which wiggled its way at a more gentle angle over the hill. I decided to avoid the traffic, and headed up the B-road. My legs weren't too good by this stage, and I puffed and panted, knees creaking, up the hill. I stopped part way for a drink, only to discover I had run out. That made the last stretch even more of a trial.

From the top though, I had a long, long downhill and I gave Scott his head, leaning into the handlebars as we built up speed.

I shouted, "Go for it, Scott."

A man, presumably a Scot, was walking his dog.

"Sorry, not you. I meant…"

At the bottom of the hill, in Braco, a lady in a shop happily filled my water bottle, and I turned off on to another minor road that would take me into Dunblane avoiding that old foe, the A9. We crossed a stream making its way south, and it occurred to me that the last hill would also have been a watershed; the water in this stream would find its way into the Firth of Forth by Edinburgh.

This was a nice road, flat along the bottom of the valley and I raised my eyes to the sky, expecting the same high grey cloud as earlier in the day. This time though, my eyes lighted on some rather ominous black clouds away to the south-east. I pushed on a bit quicker, grateful that the road was going south-west.

So it was a touch alarming when the road curved round and I suddenly found I was riding directly towards not just ominous black clouds, but a full-blown cloud burst. It was dry where I was, but just a half mile off, it was as though a curtain was being pulled across the sky. Ahead of me, it was absolutely lashing down with rain. It was blowing towards me, and I was cycling towards it. This was not good.

I stopped and pulled my waterproof jacket from a pannier.

Now sometimes I seem to engage a different and wholly illogical temperament. An ultra-optimistic one, which bears no relationship to the circumstances. I have no explanation for this. I'm sure pessimism has a lot going for it.

"It'll blow over," I said to Scott.

"No, it won't."

Scott doesn't have this same problem.

We were by a stream, with a couple of fairly meagre trees on the bank. The sky was becoming really dark, with the wall of rain rapidly approaching. It did occur to me that probably I ought to put on full waterproofs, over-trousers and the rain cover on my helmet, and to put waterproof covers over Scott's panniers.

"It won't last," I said, and I stood resolutely under the small tree with just my jacket on, as the first spatters of rain arrived.

"There is a possibility," Scott said, "that this was not your best idea."

You know if you wash vegetables through a colander, the way the water floods through the little holes and gushes in vertical streams into the sink? Imagine standing underneath the colander as the water runs through. That was what was suddenly on me, the rain simply pouring down. I can't even say it bounced off the road, because if a drop tried to bounce, it was instantly hit by the next raindrop to fall.

I scrabbled in a pannier, leaning over it to stop the rain flooding in. Out came my helmet cover, so my helmet had to come off to put the cover on. My head was streaming before I was able to fit the cover and put the helmet back on. Then I was hopping on the road-turned-river to pull waterproof trousers on, my trainers mopping up the water like sponges. I pulled overshoes on, though it was a little late really. Then covers for the panniers, and finally I was able to lean back against the trunk of the tree to take shelter.

The tree was rubbish. They don't design trees like they used to. Within seconds of the deluge arriving, the leaves of the tree had given up, hanging vertically to simply guide more water towards me. There was a branch above my head, and that was the only thing that stopped a proportion of the rain having a direct hit.

"It's an interesting tree trunk," I said to Scott.

"No, it's not."

"Please yourself."

After ten minutes, my optimism was starting to wane.

The rain eased a little, then came on even harder, the wind pushing it under the branch. I eased around the tree slightly.

It didn't help.

"There are ants sheltering under the branch," I said.

"Good for them."

Scott was more than a little wet.

The rain eased a bit more, and then got harder again.

I hummed. I think it was 'White Christmas'.

"Stop humming."

"Sorry."

A flash of colour, and two cyclists rode past, their wheels sinking deep into the flooding road. They were wearing short-sleeve bike-shirts and cycle shorts. One waved.

"That's just plain daft," I said.

I stood my ground.

Scott said, "I wonder what that the bed-and-breakfast in

Crieff was like."

Another cyclist rode past. A young woman. Cycle shorts. Bike shirt. Head down, pushing through the water.

This was becoming a little embarrassing.

"We'll go for it," I said, which was a signal for the rain to get even harder. "In a minute."

I searched the sky for a break in the darkness. For a sign.

"Optimism," Scott said, "is over-rated."

"Oh, blithering... things!" I said, and I pulled him into the road and mounted up, pushing off as the deep puddles tried to hold his tyres in place, the rain coursing down my face.

I think it was about ten miles into Stirling, crossing the A9, cycling through Dunblane and Bridge of Allan, with all the way the rain hammering on to me, cars swishing past creating the wakes of a speed-boat towing a water-skier, my cycling gloves soaked through and cold.

At the road-sign for Stirling, the rain finally steadied to no more than 'heavy'.

I got lost cycling into Stirling.

So far, I thought, I had mostly been lost cycling out of a town. Being lost within a few hundred yards of your destination in heavy rain can batter even the most profound optimist, I found.

I cycled round the ring road, with occasional views up to a grey castle on the rocky hill above. There had to be a sign for the youth hostel. There was a museum, shops and a Tourist Information Centre. Yes, I thought, I can ask in the Tourist Information Centre. I pulled in. It was closed. The streets were empty. There was not a soul to ask.

The rain was finally becoming 'moderate' as I stopped at red traffic lights. And as suddenly as it had started, the rain was gone. I stripped off my cycling gloves and squeezed one, the water streaming out through my fingers.

From behind there was a pip on a horn. I turned. A Japanese couple were grinning at me, the man with his thumb up. His lady passenger pulled out a camera and motioned with it towards my hands. I squeezed out the other glove, water spilling down again, and there was a flash. Another pip on the horn; thumbs up; grins.

"At least you've made someone happy," Scott said.

I cycled a little further round the ring road before I found someone who had been tempted outside by the drying weather – an older lady with a dog, who fortunately knew where the hostel was. It was up a steep hill on a road towards the castle. I set off, but somehow the legs were not responding. I checked the bike computer: 70 miles. Ouch, that was too far, and the steep hill was just too much. I got off and pushed. It was the first time on my ride. I didn't want to, but really, there was no choice.

As we arrived at the hostel, the sun came out. I leant Scott against the imposing Georgian frontage and peeled off my waterproofs. They had kept out the rain, but I felt awfully clammy and damp and very, very tired.

The inside of the hostel was quite different to the outside – it seemed almost brand new, with modern stairs and concrete walls, but a nice, friendly atmosphere.

The guy behind the counter checked me in with a smile. He asked where I was headed and said, "It's rough weather down in England though. Floods. And I gather it's headed this way for the day after tomorrow."

"What? The day after tomorrow?"

"That's what they say. Strong winds. Very heavy rain. Today was nothing. Apparently."

A large group of happy American twelve- and thirteen-year-olds were shepherded through the front doors behind me, giggling, and on up the stairs.

The guy behind the counter turned his attention back to me, and I wasn't sure whether it was something to do with the group of kids or tomorrow's forecast, but I recognised a knowing grin, and it was ever-so slightly worrying. I hoped it was something to do with the kids. I could do without strong winds and very heavy rain on the day I would be cycling over the Forth Road Bridge.

Captain's log: Day Eleven

Target:	44.0 miles	70.4 Km
Actual distance:	70.4 miles	112.6 Km
	(mad; quite, quite mad)	
Average speed:	12.1 mph	19.4 Kmph
Maximum speed:	29.0 mph	46.4 Kmph
Total distance:	467.7 miles	748.3 Km

I had showered, changed and been out to buy food to cook. When I came back into the hostel, the American kids were coming back down the stairs, giggling even more than before. Each of them, boys and girls, was wearing a kilt in rich red tartan, or bright blue or green, pleated and reaching to the knees, with little pale legs underneath.

All except one boy, who seemed to have found a lady's skirt. It was of unpleated, bright green tartan, and reached right down to his ankles. It wasn't a good look. I tried very hard to suppress a smile.

One of the young teachers met my eyes and shook his head slightly. "I know," he said to me.

The guy behind the counter caught my eye, and winked.

Day Twelve

Target: 26 miles / 41.6 Km
From Stirling to Aberdour
via Bannockburn and Dunfermline

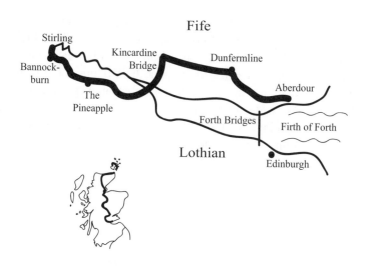

The American children were having breakfast as I came down into the comfortable dining room. There were thirty of them and they were fairly noisy, but as I sat down with a banana, a muesli bar and a yoghurt, the young teacher rose to his feet.

"Five!" he shouted.

The noise level went down slightly.

"Four!"

Quieter again.

By the time he reached One, there was silence. In a soft voice, he issued times and instructions for packing up and moving on. There were no interruptions or questions. It was all a bit impressive.

I managed to ride Scott up the remainder of the road to the castle. My legs were tired after the previous day's epic ride, but really not too bad. Maybe the ride was toughening me up. It was about time.

I had hoped this would be a quick charge round the castle, before setting off for Fife, and we were at the outer gatehouse by 9.15, in an almost empty car park. Unfortunately, the castle didn't open till 9.30, but in terms of places to wait, this was more than alright. The view over the low wall was wide and magnificent.

In the middle-distance were wooded hills and on a tree-covered promontory in the valley below rose the Wallace Monument, a dark tower amongst the greenery. The monument celebrates the life of William Wallace, the hero who gave Mel Gibson his Braveheart moment.

13th century Scotland had become a mess. England's King Edward I had seized his opportunity and pretty much ruled Scotland. The Scottish Earls had been either humiliated or killed, leaving the Scots people with nobody to lead them. Wallace began a guerrilla campaign against the English, his success bringing more support from the Scots people than from the nobles. Then he won a bloody battle here at Stirling Bridge, down in the valley below where I stood.

King Edward was not about to give up, and more campaigns over following years saw Scotland taken again by the English, with Wallace going into hiding, and then betrayed to the English. He was taken south to London, tortured, tried as a rebel against his King, and executed. His body was cut into four parts, which were displayed round the country as a warning against further rebellion.

His legacy was a changed Scottish people, a people which signed up to one of the great pieces of writing on freedom and independence, the Declaration of Arbroath, written in 1320, centuries before counterparts such as the Declaration of Independence by the United States of America. Part of it reads:

'For as long as but a hundred of us remain alive, never will we on any conditions be brought under English rule. It is in truth not for glory, nor riches, nor honours that we are fighting, but for freedom - for that alone, which no honest man gives up but with life itself.'

At half past nine a small queue formed at the first gatehouse, and two men in tartan trousers and blue jumpers began waving visitors through. I followed them in, through more gates, under a portcullis and into the massive, grey castle itself. The 13th century castle was destroyed by the Scots themselves to prevent the English using it against them, so the castle as I was seeing it was built two hundred years later, by Scottish Kings who owed their thrones to Wallace and Bruce – even if they claimed the thrones as their God-given right.

A restoration of the castle was part way through, and a magnificent new timber-beamed roof had been built over the medieval hall. Two thrones were set together underneath a coat of arms showing twin unicorns supporting the Scottish lion-rampant, red against its gold shield.

Hanging from the walls were the most beautiful tapestries. Made to centuries-old patterns, the bright reds and golds and blues of costumes and gowns spoke of their newness. In fact they were woven here in the castle, and had I been there later in the day, I could have watched more being woven. They were quite extraordinary.

I was taking the castle at a rush; I had some way to go still that day, and Stirling Castle deserved longer, but I was out with Scott again as the first coaches of the day were disgorging their visitors.

Down in the town we found cycle route signs for Bannockburn, which was good, because otherwise I might have got lost. We were directed over a pedestrian crossing, along a road, down an underpass, back up a ramp, and there I was – back where I had started. I must have gone wrong, I thought. I tried again. Over the pedestrian crossing, along the road, down the underpass, back up the ramp.

"Scott," I said, "I think we'll use the road."

The road was busy, with cars appearing at alarming angles, so when another cycle route sign for Bannockburn appeared, I followed that. I shortly found myself in the middle of a low-rise housing development, probably 1960s, judging by the sorry concrete and the flat, undecorated surfaces. It was so absolutely different to the northern Scotland I had cycled through. In the midst of the low blocks, there was a sign: 'End of Cycle Route'.

William Wallace can't have had this problem.

I gave in again, and we followed the main road, finally finding a car park and a route into the park where that other great man of Scotland's War of Independence – Robert the Bruce – had finished what Wallace had started.

Robert the Bruce was a possible heir to the Scottish throne, though with England running the country, that meant very little. Through years of battle and escape and battle again, he finally had Stirling Castle surrounded – the English garrison holding out for the arrival of Edward II from England. When the English arrived, they were met here at Bannockburn by the Scots under Robert the Bruce.

We meandered up to a small hill with a circular structure

topped off by the flag of Scotland, and I read the sign. This was where Robert the Bruce had set his standard waiting for the English.

The English were ignominiously defeated, their King just managing to escape.

The battle didn't stop English Kings from interfering and invading for the next three hundred years, but Wallace and Bruce, Stirling Bridge and Bannockburn made Scotland a different country. Perhaps they helped define Scotland.

Now there's a thought.

On the far side of the hill, a statue of Robert the Bruce stood proud on top of a tall stone plinth. It was of greened bronze, the man in armour and chain-mail on his equally chain-mailed charger, looking south for the coming of the enemy. 'Robert the Bruce, King of Scots', it said, '1306-1329'. I balanced the camera to take a timed shot and grinned at the appropriate moment. When I looked at the picture, there were Scott and I standing in front of the massive plinth, with the King of Scots looming high above, and a dark mass of clouds looming even higher behind. Time, I thought, to move on.

We wound our way back down to the visitor centre. I was going to be following my own route again, and it seemed a good idea to ask for instructions.

There were two guys chatting by the door, one in tartan trousers and jumper, the other in kilt, white shirt and steel helmet. He also had a spear.

"Excuse me," I said, "can you direct me to Cowie Road?"

"Yes," jumper-man said, "go left and back up tae the roundabout, and turn right."

The man with the spear chipped in. "Aye, don't go through the housing estate or they'll stone you."

Jumper-man looked affronted and assured me, "They won't. He's joking."

"Aye, I'm joking," he said. "But don't go through the housing estate."

We didn't go through the housing estate.

At least I had Kevlar-lined tyres though.

Once off the main road and away from the town, we were on a quiet country lane with grain fields on either side. Twin lines of enormous pylons strode through the fields, then over my head, marching from the hills north of me directly south. I wondered if this was what the lady up near Dounreay had been complaining of, Scotland's electricity being sent to England. Beyond the fields, in the middle distance, were chimneys and factories. It felt like we were on a rural island.

I was heading south-east with the River Forth on the left. If I went straight on, I would get to Edinburgh, but I had a detour to make. I couldn't cycle through Scotland without visiting Aberdour, the town in Fife where I grew up. So I was going to cross back over the Forth (by then the Firth of Forth, an estuary rather than a river) via the Kincardine Bridge, before heading east to Fife. Only then would we turn south to the Forth Road Bridge, back over the Firth of Forth and into Edinburgh, and then break for the border. Perhaps I should have headed straight there from Pitlochry, but I had wanted to go to Stirling, and was glad I had. It would have felt like a gap if I had missed it.

And then there were signs for 'The Pineapple'. I had been looking forward to this.

We turned off on to a small lane and I left Scott at a gate in a high brick wall where a couple of cars were parked. The gate led into a walled garden, with fruit trees set in an immaculate lawn. The sun was out now, and with the wind blocked by the wall and by trees beyond, it was warm. Apart from the singing of birds in those fruit trees, it was also silent.

The lawn rose off to my right, and there it was, a truly enormous stone pineapple surmounting a long, low, building. The pineapple rested on top of a hexagonal room at first floor level, stone leaves sticking out of the upper part of the walls, rising into the high dome of the pineapple itself, complete with the segments of pineapple skin all carved from stone. On the very top rested the fronds, sticking out of the pineapple into the blue above. It looked for all the world like a giant fruit at Pompeii, set rigid for all time in lava.

Built in the 18th century at a time when the pineapple was an exotic symbol of wealth, the building today belongs to the National Trust for Scotland. Apparently, it can be rented out as a holiday home.

It was distinctly, marvellously, odd.

A porch at the front must have housed the back door into the building, and there were more buildings on the far side of the pineapple. Inside the porch were two benches, and I sat for a while to rest and to refuel. It was very, very pleasant looking back down the lawn to the trees, all bathed in sunshine, and knowing that your back was resting against a building shaped exactly like a giant pineapple.

My road led into the small town of Airth. It was perfectly flat, and I was feeling good about the world, when there was a loud bang from Scott's back wheel, and we came to an involuntary stop.

I leant Scott against a tree and found that a bolt holding the frame of the back pannier had fallen off and that the end of the pannier-frame was now jammed between the gear-thingies (have I mentioned that I am mechanically-challenged?) and the frame of the bike. I tugged the pannier-frame out, but without the bolt, it just sat there on top of the gear-thingies.

I searched back along the road for the bolt, but there was no sign of it; whether it had sheered off or come loose, I had no idea, but I needed another bolt. My tool kit (well, the plastic bag that contains my medley of tools and replacement parts) was buried beneath a lot of other kit, so before long my travelling gear was distributed across the grass, which provided good entertainment for a variety of the local under-12s.

The bag had a mixture of bolts of different sizes. None of them, however, was the right fit.

There is an outside chance that I said rude word.

I did, though, have the answer, and I pulled out of the bag the cable-ties that I had been given in Thurso. One up for the mechanically-challenged, I thought, as I cable-tied the pannier-frame in place. I wasn't entirely sure how long it would last – cable-ties were probably not designed to be load-bearing – but it would do till I found a source of correct-sized bolts.

A few hundred metres along the road, I had already pedalled past a car showroom when it occurred to me that cars probably had bolts in them. I turned round and found the workshop round the side. Three guys in oily overalls were chatting in the sun as I rounded the corner.

"Hi," one said. "Can we help?"

"I was wondering if you'd have a bolt that would fit my pannier-frame."

"Aye. No problem."

He wheeled Scott off into the dark workshop and I followed him in, as did his mates. The mechanic examined the frame and vanished into the back.

"Where've yeh cycled from?" the youngest of his mates asked.

"Well, Orkney, but not today."

"Orkney? Orkney!?"

The older mechanic came back with three possible bolts.

"He's come from Orkney!" the youngster said.

"Orkney? Where're yeh finishing?"

"The border."

He considered. "Long way."

"You could do it," I said. "Just… get on a bike and go."

"Aye." He looked at me, a set of wire-cutters came out, and he clipped off the cable-tie, tightening the right-size bolt in place.

I wasn't sure whether to offer to pay, and in the end said, "Thanks. That's really brilliant. How much do I owe you?"

He looked a little affronted.

"Nothing."

"Oh, right, well, thanks very much," I said, grateful for the generosity and help.

"Where're yeh heading today?"

"Aberdour."

"Well," he said, "yeh've a braw day for it."

The main road approaching and crossing Kincardine Bridge was awful. Really awful. There were road works with just a narrow single lane and cones on either side, and a continuous stream of traffic. It was no place for a man on a bike.

I watched for a while, waiting for a gap. When one appeared, I leapt into it, and – so far as that is possible – raced off. Before long, I was conscious that all the traffic ahead of me had vanished into the distance, and that the car behind me, no doubt followed by many more, was edging closer to my back wheel.

Where a cone had been pushed out of place by a wheel, I manoeuvred off to the side, and the roar of traffic flew past me, inches away.

I waited, again, for a gap.

I repeated the process three times, all the way over the bridge. I have no idea what the Firth of Forth looked like from Kincardine Bridge. Maybe there was a wonderful view in the sunshine up towards Stirling. Then again, maybe there wasn't. I was just a bit too concerned with self-preservation at that stage to take in my surroundings.

I was heading for what I sincerely hoped was a cycleway which I had seen from the internet connected Alloa off to the west with Dunfermline to my east. So at the end of the bridge I ignored the B-road which wound around the coast, and stayed on the now un-coned, but still busy, A-road. Unfortunately, I had been unable to find a map of the cycle-lane. My theory had been that if I just headed north on this A-road, I must cross it. Must.

There were more roadworks off to the left, maybe a replacement road to this one, and there were even signs for Sustrans Cycle Route 76, but they were all heading west, back towards Stirling. I desperately wanted a Route 76 sign heading east for Dunfermline to get me off the main road. Perhaps the cycleway hadn't been finished yet, or the signs not put in place. Either way, I didn't find it.

After a couple of miles, we came on another A-road sign-posted for Dunfermline, and it became clear that I had missed the cycleway altogether. Coming on top of the scary crossing of the Kincardine Bridge, this was not my best moment. I was tired. I was hungry. And it's also possible that I was grumpy.

It was another three or so miles of main road before a shop had a sign for sandwiches made to order. A café might have been preferable, but I asked the lady for a sandwich and whether there was a bench where I could sit to eat it.

She made the sandwich and said, no, there was no bench where I could sit to eat it.

So I wrapped the sandwich up and put it in a pannier, possibly in a grumpy sort of way, though I can't be sure of that, and we cycled off.

Just a hundred metres down the road, we came to a new little piece of garden apparently designed to improve the ex-mining village, and there were several little benches.

I sat and ate my sandwich.

I was still grumpy.

What I really needed, I decided, was a decent amount of caffeine, so when the road took us on into Dunfermline, I did seem to gravitate towards a café that looked as though it might do a mean cappuccino. The café was opposite the Tourist Information Centre, and I wandered in for directions to the Abbey.

She showed me on a map and said, "You can keep that."

"No, it's OK."

"Ah, you'll not want the extra weight on your bike."

It occurred to me that finding my way might take precedence over the extra weight of a small piece of paper.

"Well, perhaps I will keep the map," I said. "Thank you."

I noticed various places named after Andrew Carnegie – the park, the library and so on. Apparently this son of Dunfermline had made his fortune in the steel trade in America, and as well as paying for libraries across the country, he had determined to improve the lives of those he had left behind in the weaving town of Dunfermline. He had bought a rich estate in town, for example, and turned the grounds into a public park.

Scott and I bumped down a little hill to the Abbey, guided by my new map. There was something to be said, I thought, for not being lost in a town. It was, generally speaking, a good experience, and one that would be nice to repeat.

A sign outside the Abbey said that there was free entry to the church, so I wandered in through the thick oak door.

Inside, the floor was of stone, seeming to absorb whatever light there was at ground level. Heavy, round pillars rose out of the gloom to support three levels of Norman arches, the upper two levels golden with light.

There was a lady attendant watching me, and I said, "Can I take photos?"

"Yes, you can, but you have to buy a ticket to come in."

"The sign outside said it was free."

"That's for the church." She indicated a doorway further up the church, underneath a huge window, through which more golden light was filtering. "The other half of the building."

"So this isn't the church?"

"No. You have to pay for this part. The ticket office is over there."

She bustled away, and a voice behind me said, "I wouldn't worry."

I turned and found an older lady there, glasses perched on her nose as she looked at me.

"No, well, I was only going to be a couple of minutes. I was just amazed by the Norman columns and arches."

"Yes," she said. "Apparently they were built by the same mason that built Durham Cathedral."

"I can believe it. They're amazing. Tell me, are you a visitor or do you live in Dunfermline?"

"I live here. I've lived here all my life, and I often come in." She smiled an impish smile. "I don't pay though."

"And the church is through there?" I pointed to the door.

"Yes, do go on in. It's well worth it."

"I will," I said. "And I expect I'll make a small donation." She smiled again. "That would be kind."

The church half of the Abbey was quite different, bright with light and with people, specifically a party of Americans surrounding the pulpit to listen to their guide.

Underneath the pulpit was the tomb of Robert the Bruce himself, he of the victory at Bannockburn and of the almost-legendary-Robert-the-Bruce-Burger in Pitlochry.

The Americans were very impressed, though probably more with the former than the latter.

The church was certainly free to go in, which I considered absolutely right and proper, and I did leave a small donation, feeling slightly less grumpy with the world than before.

I got lost cycling out of Dunfermline.

This was so unfair. I had a map. It should be obvious.

"You're lost, aren't you?" Scott said.

"No. Well, slightly."

"Slightly, as in, you have no idea where you are?"

I chanced upon a purpose-built cycle lane next to the road to Dalgety Bay, wide and smooth and easy to ride. The afternoon was wearing on, and there seemed to people cycling home from work as well as kids playing. Maybe, I thought, it was well used because it had been so well designed.

The cycle lane led me in its wide and smooth way directly into Dalgety Bay, and from there I knew I could drop down to the coast to pick up my old ally from Orkney and northern Scotland – Cycle Route 1 – as it made its way from Edinburgh up to Aberdeen and from there to Inverness. It ought, really, to be simple.

I got lost cycling out of Dalgety Bay.

"I'm saying nothing," Scott said.

We were in a genteel little housing estate of modern bungalows and semis. I knew that behind them there was a cycle route. In fact I could see the coast between houses, and I did contemplate tossing Scott over a well-manicured six-foot hedge in the vague direction of the sea. Mind you, I wasn't sure if that was anything to do with finding the cycle route.

Just up the hill, a lady was weeding her front garden, and I pedalled over to her.

"Excuse me," I said, "can you tell me how to get to the cycle route to Aberdour?"

"Yes, of course. Where are you going to in Aberdour?"

"Shore Road."

"My mother-in-law lived round the corner from Shore Road for many years."

"We lived on Shore Road when I was little, though it's a bit of a long time ago now."

I had been a newborn baby when my dad was posted to Rosyth Dockyard up the coast from here. My mum had followed him with my three older brothers and myself as a two-month old baby, all the way from Plymouth. It must have been an epic journey, followed by more epic journeys over the next seven (pre-motorway) years as they travelled to and from family in Kent for Christmas and holidays.

The lady smiled. "When would it have been?"

"It's actually about forty years since we left."

"I wonder if you will think it's changed at all? Now, the cycle route is just over there – between the houses."

"Easy. Thank you."

It was easy as well, into the woods and on to an old railway-line cycleway, across a lane, and then I was cycling past Aberdour Golf Course on its grassy slope leading down to the sea.

I remembered a snowy winter at the golf course, with all four brothers squashed on to a wooden sled, picking up speed down the slope, dropping into a snow-covered bunker and hitting the far wall, tumbling off into deep, soft, cold whiteness. How old was I? I don't know. Less than seven, but memories really don't have ages.

The cycleway joined a road and then I was on Shore Road itself, dropping down the hill to where the road swung left immediately above the beach. I pulled in outside the first house I remember living in.

It was an older, semi-detached, stone house, with large windows. Steps led up from the road so that the views out to sea over the beach must be grand. I remembered the interwoven railings at the front, but possibly more from a photo of me in the front garden, aged about four, sitting there with our dog, Lassie, and wearing a jumper with pinned-on badges down the front. Perhaps it was my birthday, and the badges each said, 'Happy Birthday!' or perhaps as a four-year-old, I was into my badges. I can't remember now, though I wish I could.

I had been happy here, and I remembered playing with toy soldiers or cars right there in the garden, usually with my friend Gavin.

And I remembered the beach. Today, the tide was in, and it was just a narrow strip of sand curving around the bay and shelving steeply into choppy dark waters. Little waves rushed in, breaking amongst odd clumps of seaweed and rocks.

I left Scott by a bench on the grass at the side of the road and walked down to the beach, feeling the freshness of the wind, tasting and smelling the salt. We used to dare each other to jump down on to the sand from some impossible height, maybe about, oh, five foot. We were six years old, and our bravery clearly knew no bounds.

Away across the Firth, grey shadows suggested the hills behind Edinburgh. Closer was the island of Inchcolm, a little place of grass and rock which I remembered visiting in a boat from the beach here, having adventures amongst the ruins of the Abbey, or playing pirates on our own desert island.

Along at the far end of the road a slipway ran down into the harbour, and little boats swung on anchors. Across the far side of the harbour, woods lined a low hillside. Somewhere beyond, I remembered, lay Silver Sands, a place for a children's picnic on a sunny day out, with buckets and spades, and sand in your sandwiches.

I walked back to Scott past the old red wartime mine on the sea-front, even now a collection point for 'distressed sailors', and looked up again at the house. I had wondered if this would feel like coming home, and I had my answer. It was more like meeting an old friend who you haven't seen for years; recalling good times, but not really knowing each other at all. Not really.

I dialled a familiar number on my phone.

"Hi Mum."

"Oh, hello, Michael."

"I just thought I'd let you know that I'm standing outside our old house on Shore Road."

"Has it changed?"

"Hardly at all, I think. Though it's a bit hard to remember."

"Can you see Inchcolm?"

"Yes, though it's a bit gloomy."

"Well, if you had our weather here, you wouldn't even see Inchcolm. Did you know that this rain will be with you tomorrow?"

"Oh?"

"Yes. Torrential, apparently. There's been quite a bit of flooding."

"Oh."

"When is Richard joining you?"

Richard, my son, was to cycle with me for the last part of the journey, just as he had done when I had cycled across England.

"Tomorrow. I'm cycling across the Forth Bridge tomorrow, and he's coming up to Edinburgh on the train to meet me."

"It's going to be very windy as well. Stormy. Not the best for your cycling."

"Mm. Especially on the bridge."

I cycled back up the hill and into the drive of my guesthouse, set back behind trees in Victorian splendour. The lady-owner welcomed me into a large hall with a double-staircase and a stripped-wood floor. There were antique cabinets and paintings lit by gentle lighting.

"This is wonderful," I said.

She smiled. "We like it."

Captain's log: Day Twelve

Target:	26.0 miles	41.6 Km
Actual distance:	40.0 miles	64.0 Km
	(possibly a fairly serious	
	map-reading error?)	
Average speed:	10.3 mph	16.5 Kmph
Maximum speed:	25.0 mph	40.0 Kmph
Total distance:	507.7 miles	812.3 Km
	(500 miles; that felt like	
	a landmark)	

I found an extremely filling pie and chips in a pub up in the village that night, washed down with an acceptable pint of the brown stuff. So I was in a relaxed mood when, on the way back into the guest house, my host stopped me.

"Have you seen the weather forecast for tomorrow? It's going to be the wettest day of the year. And so windy. The bridge might well be closed. Which way are you cycling?"

"Over the bridge."

She hesitated. "Well, sometimes they're wrong."

Day Thirteen

Target: 34 miles / 54.4 Km
From Aberdour to Roslin
via the Forth Road Bridge and Edinburgh

The sun wasn't exactly streaming in through the window, but there was enough light to see across the fluffy duvet to the tea-and-coffee-making facilities, and to remind me that this was most definitely not a hostel. Downstairs, cooked breakfast was probably underway. Then there was the double bed. Was it just comfortable, or was it luxurious? A hard decision. Perhaps I should lay there and consider the answer for a little longer.

A splatter of rain rattled the window and last night's weather forecast came into my head. I pottered across the room and pulled back the curtains on doomsday. A tree in the garden was lurching wildly from side to side. Bucketloads of rain were being flung past the window by unseen hands from somewhere off to the left.

I dropped the curtain, flicked the switch on the kettle, switched on the television, and got back into bed. The bed was probably luxurious, but I was prepared to try it out a little longer. Just to be certain.

The weather forecast came on. "South East Scotland will have the worst of the weather today. Expect very heavy rain and very strong winds all day. Gusts will exceed -"

I pulled the covers over my head.

I had about 18 miles to cycle to the middle of Edinburgh, where Richard would be meeting me at the station. From there we would cycle on to Roslin to another guest house. It was a short day, and I was really looking forward to meeting up with him. But would the bridge be open? And if it was open, would it be safe on the bike? Then there was Richard. If it was this wet and windy, it wouldn't be too much fun for him either.

I decided I had three options.

> 1. Go for it. Battle the winds. Get wet. Make it across the bridge. Meet Richard as planned. Plough on regardless.
> 2. Cycle as far as Edinburgh (if the bridge was open) and tell Richard to get a later train. We would stay the

night there and carry on tomorrow, when hopefully, the storm would have blown itself out.

3. Put everything back a day. Tell Richard to come up tomorrow instead. At least I would have a chance to decide if the bed really was luxurious.

I dithered.

I phoned home and dithered a bit on the phone.

"The weather's not too bad here," Claire said. "You'll have to decide."

Over a definitely-luxurious cooked breakfast, my host confirmed the weather forecast. "It's really stormy out there."

"Do you have a spare room for tonight if I decide to put everything back a day?"

"Yes, of course."

I poked my head out the front door. It was pretty awful. But I had cycled this far across Scotland. Surely a bit of weather wouldn't put me off. Surely.

I decided to go for it.

I phoned home again and spoke to Richard. "Let's go for it," I said.

Back in the bedroom I put on every waterproof item I possessed, zipped or poppered every possible means for water to get inside, and pulled everything tight. By the time I was finished, I could hardly move.

I lumbered downstairs and went round the back of the house to retrieve Scott. Putting the panniers on involved bending, and that wasn't easy.

"Doctor Who Monsters are more bendable than you."

"Huh."

I brought him out of the shed, and then wheeled him round the front of the house, scrunching on the gravel. I looked up. It was funny, but now that all the gear was on, the rain felt much less hard.

"Scott," I said. "The rain's nearly stopped."

"So are we going for optimism then?"

"No."

I pedalled out on to the road, where the rain stopped altogether, and a feeble sun broke through.

I may have said a rash word.

The Doctor Who Monster got lost cycling out of Aberdour, and since we were retracing my route to Dalgety Bay, this was a little disappointing.

It was probably Scott's fault.

I found a postman. "Can you tell me where the cycle route to Dalgety Bay goes?"

"You're on it."

I cycled back past the golf course and through the woods. I was very, very hot, but I was determined not to succumb to false optimism. As I'd heard a manager of a doomed football club say at the end of a season, it's the hope that kills you. Much better to have no hope at all. I would hold on firmly to a grim fatalism; it could still be, I thought, a doomed attempt to cross the bridge in a hurricane.

"The wind's dropped," Scott said.

"Oh shut up."

The detached houses and bungalows of Dalgety Bay's shore-hugging housing estate spread right down almost to the water, their tidy and bright gardens a contrast to the rocky coast. There was a steadily lightening view towards Inchcolm, and beyond that, across the Firth of Forth, to Edinburgh. I finally gave up on my pessimism; there was a limit to how long I could keep it up. In the end, it was quite a relief to strip off the waterproofs and to pack them away. I exchanged clear glasses for sunglasses, and set off.

And then I was lost again. I was not happy. I had only cycled about three miles and been lost twice already. I had been following Route 1 signs, but maybe looking at the view opening up to the two Forth Bridges had distracted me. Now I was in a turning circle at the end of a cul-de-sac, smart houses on the right, sea on the left, and a path ahead of me with a sign that said 'PRIVATE WAY – NO VEHICLES'. Somewhere behind me, a Route 1 sign must have led off into the housing estate.

A car reversed into the turning circle, and I pedalled over to him.

"Excuse me," I said, as he wound the window down. "I've lost the cycle route."

"The proper route is up there," he said, gesturing beyond the houses, "but just go that way."

He pointed past the signpost.

"It says 'Private Way'. Is that OK?"

"Sure."

When our kids were young, they liked to play football on the grass outside our house, using as a goalpost the 'NO UNAUTHORISED BALLGAMES' sign. When they were old enough to understand what 'UNAUTHORISED' meant, I explained and then I 'AUTHORISED' their ballgame.

So no problem there then.

This felt a bit like that. Some guy reversing into a turning circle had just 'AUTHORISED' my cycling along a 'Private Way'.

So no problem there then.

I'm not sure why, but it really didn't occur to me that there might be a practical reason, rather than a legal reason, why this was not the cycle route. Not until I was pushing a bouncing and heavily-laden Scott down steep steps, and then pushing the same heavily-laden Scott back up another set of steep steps. It was wet and muddy underfoot from the overnight rain, and my feet were feeling distinctly damp. My feet weren't helped when I realised that I had taken my sunglasses off at the start of the pushing, and that I was no longer wearing them; I walked back down and up the steps until I found them.

The day hadn't started particularly well.

Route 1 signs reappeared, and I pedalled along a grassy coastline towards the two iconic bridges. Closest was the original Forth Bridge, with its three humps of interlinking iron, a red-painted Loch Ness monster striding across the estuary. Beyond, a set of pillars bearing the weight of the Forth

Road Bridge stood proud, the cables of the suspension bridge curving down to an out-of-sight carriageway.

Two weeks before, the rail bridge had carried my train northwards for the start of the journey. To be about to cycle back across the Forth Road Bridge seemed something of an achievement.

Just downstream, a liner was moored, much like the one I had seen off the Black Isle, shining somehow white in a day that was darkening again as cloud rolled up from the south. The sun was gone now, and the wind had returned. I shivered. It would be chilly on the bridge and I pulled my jacket out of a pannier. I'd be glad to be the other side of the bridge if that rain was coming back.

A hill took us up through Inverkeithing away from the water, following signs for the Forth Road Bridge, and then suddenly we were being shepherded on to a wide cycle lane leading straight ahead towards those bridge pillars. Traffic boomed past on the carriageway, but the cycle lane was empty and inviting. We rose gently on to the bridge itself and I stopped to take in the view of the rail bridge, a thing of beauty, as it made its way across the Forth. Some of the struts had white shrouds around them, and I wondered if it was true that painting the Forth Bridge was a never-ending task, finishing one end only to find that the other end needed painting again.

At the highest point of the curve of the bridge, I stopped again. The waters of the Forth were a long way below. Beyond was Edinburgh stretching away towards the castle on its rock above the city centre, and behind it the old volcano of Arthur's Seat.

A lady of middle years and sensible clothes was walking towards me from the Edinburgh side of the bridge.

"Hi," I said. "I wonder, would you mind taking a photo of me on my camera?"

"Of course. Is it your first time on the bridge?"

"Well, it's just that I've cycled from the Orkney Islands and this feels like a big moment, cycling across the Forth Road

Bridge."

"Pass me the camera," she said.

I looked at the photo after she had gone. Me in my blue and black jacket fastened against the wind, with a black cycling helmet and something of a smile; Scott with bright yellow pannier-covers at the back, a map tucked into the front pannier; and behind us, the Forth Bridge and the low hills of Fife. I also noticed the weather in the photograph. No rain. No gales. No storms. I was mighty pleased that I had ignored the weather forecast and hadn't whimped out.

I sent a text to Niall: "On Forth Road Bridge. How's Cornwall?"

A reply came back at once: "Wet. Finished though. And well done you."

I pushed off and free-wheeled down the slope, feet out of pedals, 'woo-hooo!' coming from me, apparently. A face in the back window of a car gave me a strange look, and I really didn't care.

At the far end of the bridge, the Route 1 signs took me off into the housing estates of Queensferry, jigging across junctions, before leaving the houses behind and finding fields again on either side. I had about ten miles to the station in Edinburgh where I would be meeting Richard, and I was looking forward to that more than I think I had admitted to myself till now.

The outer limits of Edinburgh brought more housing estates, some posh and some less so, large houses hidden behind closed gates, rows of smaller houses higgledy-piggledy together. Then my signs suddenly dropped me down on to a converted railway line, flat, tarmac'd and smooth, a perfect cycleway, without a single other cyclist on it. At first it was a joy, but after a mile or so, I realised I was seeing nothing. The cycleway was lower than its surroundings, banks of shrubs and grass on either side, and I could really have been anywhere. It was a safe and fast way of getting from one place to another on a bike, but I wanted to see Edinburgh.

As the cycleway ran out on to roads, the city finally appeared in all its glory. There were wide avenues surrounded by grand Georgian houses in elegant stone. Eglinton Crescent had a small tree-filled park in the centre. Its crescent of houses were five storeys high, including their attic rooms and their basements, but the proportions were so right and the street so wide that they just seemed the perfect size.

This was the New Town, and I pedalled on through Melville Street and Charlotte Square past more grand houses, high churches and statues and on into the wide shopping avenue of George Street, with its cafés, shops and restaurants, tourists standing and staring, cars nudging past, and pedestrians filling the pavements.

The New Town was an eighteenth century construction. The city of Edinburgh had grown upwards in the streets around the Royal Mile, between Edinburgh Castle at the top of the hill on my right, and Holyrood House tucked under the high grass-and-rock hill of Arthur's Seat. Tenement buildings had risen high above the streets, and the medieval clutter at ground-level left Edinburgh known as 'Auld Reekie' (Old Smoky) to its inhabitants. But eighteenth century new-town building had evidently created something considerably better than twentieth century new towns. The Georgian town-houses of Edinburgh were fabulous, the streets wide and airy.

With some roads cobbled, I bumped around, watching out for cars, glimpsing the castle through gaps. A right turn down Hanover Street, with the tall columns of the Royal Scottish Academy ahead of me – part of the reason for Edinburgh being known as The Athens of the North – and I was at the shopping mecca of Princes Street underneath the looming castle above, waiting for a gap in traffic, crossing between buses, knees straining to carry me up the short sharp Mound, and then down into Waverley Station. Taxis disgorged hurrying passengers, and I wheeled Scott into the concourse.

"Hey!"

Richard.

I balanced Scott against a pillar and we hugged.

(I should be clearer on that; I hugged Richard, not Scott.)

It was so good to see him (Richard, that is). It was two weeks since I had left home, and here was a part of home coming to me.

Claire had given Richard sandwiches for both of us, so we found a bench in the busy concourse, I bought a coffee, and we sat and talked about the ride, about home. People hurried and waited all around us, the garbled announcements sending them off or stalling them, but we seemed to be in a bubble, real life with us here, some other world beyond.

I pulled out the next map for the journey to show Richard. We would still be on Cycle Route 1 (apart from a planned detour today, and therefore a reasonable chance of getting lost), but this section had a name: 'Coast & Castles'. The route started here in Edinburgh, wound up into the hills to the south, past the abbeys and towns of the Borders, and dropped down to the border itself near Berwick upon Tweed. The detour was that we were finishing the day at Roslin, some twenty miles further on. I wanted to be there before the chapel closed for the day – Rosslyn Chapel made famous by the finale of 'The Da Vinci Code', and built by the Sinclairs. Yes, my ancestors had a hand in the Da Vinci Code. Perhaps I could claim royalties.

I checked the map again. The village of Pencaitland, home of the Glenkinchie distillery (*'Flowery start, complex flavours, and a dry finish. A restorative, especially after a walk in the hills'*) was too far off the route.

After too long, probably, it was time to set off.

Richard said, "Didn't you say you wanted to go in the castle or Holyrood House?"

I checked my watch and thought about it. I had been in both before. Edinburgh Castle had those views across the city, the massive walls and the Scottish crown jewels; Holyrood House had the royal apartments with wide staircases and tapestries. It had been home to Mary Queen of Scots, and was where she had witnessed the murder of her friend Rizzio by her husband. I could remember the blood-stained wooden floor shown as evidence. They were powerful places, full of the history I could be passionate about. But not for today.

"We might miss Rosslyn Chapel if we do, and I'd rather make sure we get there in time. Is that OK with you?"

"Sure. Wherever you want to go."

"Just keep an eye out for the Holy Grail when you're there."

The bubble popped, and we stepped into the other world, pushing our bikes through the mêlée towards the traffic of Edinburgh. We picked up Route 1 signs and headed up over the brow of the hill to cross the Royal Mile. Up to the right in the direction of the castle were the tenement buildings that had pre-dated the New Town, many of their ground floors now tourist shops selling cashmere, or tartan hats, or whisky. To the left were more Georgian buildings, and beyond that, out of sight, would be Holyrood House and the controversially designed Scottish Parliament building.

We dropped down on the far side of the Royal Mile, with the route leading through the open park of the Meadows, and then twisting and turning through the streets underneath the green hill of Arthur's Seat in Holyrood Park, with its cliff of stone at the top. We were heading away from the city centre, taking it in turns to lead, skimming ahead of each other, grinning. There was a tunnel, lighted but still deliciously dark to steam through, flat railway paths, cycle lanes past St Margaret's University, and then we were beyond the outskirts of Edinburgh, green fields on either side.

A new road was being built, complete with its own cycle lane, though just now there was a wide expanse of dried mud, and we cycled nonchalantly towards it side by side. So, by the time we realised that it was not dried mud, but wet, gloopy mud, two or three inches deep, we were both in it, the mud clinging and gripping on our tyres and wheels.

"Don't stop!" I shouted, forcing the pedals round to make some headway. "Don't put your foot down in it!"

I was rather hoping it wasn't cement.

We both pulled our ways through, coming out on dry ground. I stopped and examined Scott. His wheels and tyres were completely matted in the gloop. They were really quite disgusting.

"Ah," I said.

Scott said nothing.

"Dad, there's a big puddle over there."

"That'll do it."

We cycled back and forth through it, spray flying up, and after a few runs, you could at least see the tyres.

We rode on into Dalkeith town centre, with my bike computer saying 12 miles since Edinburgh and my body asking for fuel. Dalkeith had a proper high street, busy with cars and shoppers. Time was moving on, so we chained the bikes to a lamppost and bought drinks and chocolate biscuits for a quick bit of fuel and set off again.

Signposts led us on to another old railway line past Bonnyrigg. The Route 1 signs then took a left, but we carried straight on, the cycle path heading towards our destination, Roslin. With woods and fields on either side, the old railway line was a straight, flat route, though without the expected sign that would take us across to Roslin and its chapel. We weren't exactly lost, but, well, when we came on a group of walkers, I did stop and ask them if we had missed the turn.

"No, no. Carry on here, then turn off right. There is a sign."

There was a sign – to Roslin Country Park, Rosslyn Castle and Rosslyn Chapel. We turned on to a road that twisted steeply downhill, but was blocked where a landslip had taken half the road away. A man was walking up from it.

"Don't worry," he said, "you can bump your bikes around it."

He was right, and we flew down the side of the beautifully wooded valley to the bottom of the hill and then we climbed right back up the far side. This seemed to be Roslin Country Park, and it looked a tremendous place to walk and explore.

Not today; we followed signs for the Chapel and turned into a car park.

I had expected a little country chapel, with maybe the odd visitor, but no, I counted thirty cars in the car park.

"It's going to be busy," I said.

"Could be something to do with 'The Da Vinci Code'."

"Could be."

The chapel had a shop, a small café and a ticket office, and that sounds tacky, but it wasn't. It was restrained and careful.

Information boards gave a potted history of the chapel. It was built by a Sinclair – William St Clair, the 'last Prince of Orkney'.

"Do you realise," I said to Richard, "that he might be an ancestor? Your great grandmother was a Sinclair."

"Really?"

"Really."

The boards also gave some inkling of the extraordinary images inside and outside the chapel. As well as Christian carvings, there were pagan symbols, such as the 'Green Man' made of roots, leaves and branches and representing a pre- or non-Christian religious belief. In fact, Rosslyn Chapel had more 'Green Men' than in any other Medieval building, which felt very odd. Then there were the carvings related to the Knights Templar and Freemasons that had helped inspire the chapel's use in 'The Da Vinci Code'.

We passed on through into the churchyard to find that the outside of the chapel was surrounded by protective coverings on scaffolding. It was a shame, but the inside made up for it. Just walking in the door, we could see that almost every stone surface was filled with carvings.

There were a good few people in the church (and I heard what sounded like Swedish and American accents), but everyone was quiet and respectful. It still felt like a church, though a very odd one.

A young woman in uniform was starting a talk and tour, and we followed her in a group as she pointed out the eccentricities and oddities of the carvings around the roof and on the pillars, such as Lucifer, the fallen angel, hanging upside down, wings outstretched, ropes around his body.

She also told the legend that the Holy Grail is hidden underneath the chapel. "But nobody knows," she said. "The chapel still belongs to the Sinclairs, and they have ancestors buried in the vaults and so won't agree to them being opened. The vaults have been closed for 250 years."

Back outside, we climbed a ladder to a viewpoint on the scaffolding, but the coverings and scaffolding itself didn't help the view, so we went back in for a last look.

"Quite a place," I said, "and if he was an ancestor, that last Prince of Orkney is quite a guy in the family tree."

"Bit odd."

"Come on," I said. "Let's find where we're staying. I could murder a cup of tea."

A friendly couple at our B&B showed us to a comfortable room in their converted bungalow, and made us tea in the dining room. All round the room, hanging on walls or resting on stands, were musical instruments.

"Do you play all of these?" I asked our host.

"Mostly the bagpipes for a ceilidh band. Scots and Northumbrian pipes."

Northumbrian. Yes, although we were only a little south of Edinburgh, two days of cycling would get us to the border and into Northumbria. England. The end of the ride.

But first, I had two cycling days with Richard. Cycling across Scotland had been an adventure, and it felt absolutely right to share the last part of the journey with my son. I was looking forward to it.

Captain's log: Day Thirteen

Target:	34.0 miles	54.4 Km
Actual distance:	41.2 miles	65.9 Km
Average speed:	10.0 mph	16.0 Kmph
Maximum speed:	24.5 mph	39.2 Kmph
Total distance:	548.9 miles	878.2 Km

Lights out. Richard across the room.

"Rich," I said.

"Yeh."

"I've been thinking. We're at least part Sinclair. You could bury me in the vaults at Rosslyn Chapel. In the fullness of time, of course."

He said slowly, "OK."

"And you could have a little scout around while you're there."

Silence.

"You're looking for a cup."

Day Fourteen

Target: 39 miles / 62.4 Km
From Roslin to Melrose
via Innerleithen and Abbotsford

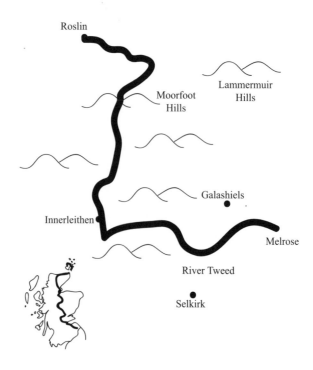

We got lost cycling out of Roslin.

How could we possibly be lost? I had a map. Two maps. Though maybe that was the problem, because I hadn't been able to match up the two maps. I had printed them off the internet and they had always been just a little skimpy on detail. The maps had also by now spent over 500 miles in a pannier joggling up and down, and they were a touch faded and creased.

We cycled back down the road into the valley and up the hill through the woods, past the landslip on to the cycleway.

"Rich," I said, showing him the maps. "I'm not a hundred per cent sure where we are on this cycleway. Look, we need to find this lane to get across to Carrington to pick up Route 1 again. But I'm not sure whether to carry on further on the cycleway or head back."

He took the maps from me, compared them and handed them back.

"No idea," he said.

"Thanks."

I looked back down the cycleway, and forward up the cycleway. They seemed pretty much the same.

"Let's carry on."

After about half a mile, there was an exit on to a road, so we took that, cycling down the road confidently until we found ourselves back on the road with the landslip.

"Rubbish!" I said. I think it was that, though from the way Richard looked at me, it might have been a different word.

"Sorry," I said.

A dog-walker examined our maps, gave up, and volunteered some very simple instructions as to how reach Carrington.

Easy, really.

There was an enormous puddle completely covering the lane leading to Carrington. It was in a dip, the grassy meadows on either side draining the recent downpours into its depths.

We both stopped.

"It's deep," I said.

"And wide."

"It'll clean our wheels."

"Good point."

Richard edged out into it and kept going as it reached the bottom of his pedals on each down stroke, then gradually eased out on to dry road on the far side.

I turned Scott around and cycled back up the road slightly.

"What are you doing?" Richard called.

"Getting a run up."

"What?"

I eased Scott round.

"YEEEHAAAA!"

I set off at speed and lifted my feet high in front as I hit the water, sending up a satisfying curtain of water before the flood slowed me and I had to pedal the rest to get across.

"I can't believe you just did that."

I looked down at my bike shirt, leggings and trainers. No, I couldn't really believe I had either. I was pretty wet. Still, it was fun though.

He was laughing. "I didn't even get a photo. You'll have to do it again."

"Again?"

"Yeh."

He was reaching round to my backpack and extracting the camera.

I cycled back through a little more sedately, up the slope on the far side.

"Ready!" he shouted.

"I can't believe I'm about to do it again."

"Go on then."

I pushed off.

"YEEEHAAA!"

I got my own back a half mile further on, where another deep puddle completely covered the road.

"Wait there," I said, cycling carefully through. Yes, it was nice and deep.

I got the camera out.

"Ready!"

He stood up on the pedals and hit the water hard.

"YEEEHAAA!"

When he came to a stop by me, he was entirely spattered with water droplets, including his face, with its broad grin.

Shortly afterwards, we found Carrington and some Route 1 signs, which was a bit of a relief. The signs pointed us south along a country lane, which dropped prettily down through woods to a grand stone bridge over what my map named the River South Esk. A plaque said that the bridge had been paid for by the First Baron of The Exchequer in the nineteenth century. It did seem a little excessive for the size of the river, but then he probably claimed it on expenses.

We cycled past walled grounds, with the odd glimpse inside of a big house, presumably that of a former First Baron of The Exchequer, and then we started climbing. I had been hoping to coast downhill all the way from my highest point in the Cairngorms, but it seemed my brother was right. The Southern Uplands were not a figment of his imagination.

The route looked a good one on the map though. Amongst the climbing, there would be one long, long hill, taking us up over the Moorfoot Hills, with a note on the map of 'Superb view towards Edinburgh from here'. After that, it looked as though the road found its way through the valleys, and was possibly mostly downhill. Still, we would see.

To begin with, the lane climbed gently, lifting us slowly out of cow-pastures and woods into rough sheep grass. There was no traffic at all, not even many farms. Very little to disturb the sheep or the birds.

"Rich," I said. "See those black and white birds with the long red beaks. They're oyster-catchers. I've been seeing them off and on all ride."

We stopped and watched my journey's mascots poking

long beaks into soft, marshy ground, and listened to their mewing whistles.

"Oyster-catchers?"

"Yes. Bit confused, these ones. Not a lot of oysters up here."

As we climbed, there were the beginnings of a view northwards. First it was across tufted sheep-country to a low green ridge, with a darker line of hills poking up from behind. Then the road turned south-west, running up the north face of the Moorfoot Hills. It was a narrow lane, straight and steep for nearly two miles. We toiled up, and at each breathless stop (breathless for me anyway – Richard wasn't suffering quite as much, which was most unfair) the view opened up further. Just before the top of the ridge, we stopped for drinks and biscuits, leaning the bikes against fences in long grass, sheep nibbling away just below on the hillside.

The view was an awesome one. One hundred and eighty degrees of air and light. On the left, the ground fell away to a valley of woods and farms before rising to a ridge of green hills. Swinging the eyes right there was a more distant line of hills, larger, bluer. These must have been across in Fife, because looking further right, the Firth of Forth came into view in front of them. It was a long sliver of silver, broken by the heights within Edinburgh – the Castle Hill and Arthur's Seat, so clearly old volcanoes from their distinctive shape. Then there were the suburbs and villages around Edinburgh, and right again the distinctive island of Inchcolm in the firth. Two large vessels were also clear, though whether tankers or Royal Navy ships or cruise liners, it was too far to tell. Further right, the firth grew wider and the coast of Fife narrower as it led off to the horizon with a blending of blue land, silver water and platinum cloud.

The road turned full south, and with a last climb we were breaking through the top of the ridge, my muscles and joints complaining. I pulled over, and Richard joined me.

"I have a theory," I said.

"What's that?"

"Well, you know you get up hills much quicker and easier than me?"

"Yep."

"That's your better Power to Weight Ratio, I reckon. 'P.W.R.' Strong muscles, low weight."

"OK."

"But when we set off down steep hills, not pedalling, I whiz past you. Well, I reckon that's 'P.H.R.' "

"P.H.R.?"

"Pasty to Height Ratio. The more pasties you've eaten and the higher you are, the faster you go. Like this."

I pushed off, freewheeling, picking up speed, Richard pedalled hard alongside me, but within seconds I was pulling away from him. A few more seconds and he was seriously lagging behind, without my turning the pedals.

"Hey Rich," I shouted back, the wind whistling past me, "EAT MORE PASTIES!"

His answer was lost in the distance. It might possibly have been something about the all-encompassing theory of P.H.R. deserving the Nobel Prize for Science, but then again, it might not.

Having cycled uphill for two miles, we now had two miles downhill, and it was wonderful. I graciously used my brakes to allow Richard to catch up, and we cycled together down the road, watched by fluffy white sheep grazing the green hills on either side.

The road levelled out in an almost straight valley, with the hills drawing closer on either side. The road appeared to be sloping downhill, yet we were having to pedal, and I couldn't blame any wind. Somehow, the hills drawing in were giving the optical illusion of a sloping road.

The map showed the hills to be quite respectable – Eastside Heights at 593m, Whitehope Law at 621m – and they looked to be good walking country, rounded and empty.

215

Farmsteads and houses began to appear, and then the road dropped again and I caught a glimpse of a cross and flowers out of the corner of an eye, and swung round to investigate.

It was a small oblong stone set on end in the ground, with a white cross seemingly freshly painted on the front, against a black background. On the cross was written, 'The Piper's Grave'. Pink flowers grew on one side, with artificial yellow flowers on the other.

Later I found 'The Piper's Grave' on the internet. The story is that in the 18th century, a famed piper made a bet with some friends over a few drinks that he could play the bagpipes all the way from Innerleithen, just ahead of us, to Edinburgh Castle. They all set off, but the 'friends' had made a small hole in his bagpipes, and the extra puffing did for the piper. This, apparently, was as far as he got.

The grave was clearly tended, and important to someone, here in this quiet, narrow valley.

We set off again, freewheeling down by a growing stream. Sheep ambled across the road, and we slowed frequently to avoid tumbling over them. Heather and fern crept down to the road with its over-ambitious white line down the middle, the heather with a first bloom of purple, the ferns a bright, clear green.

Then we were coasting past plantations, and arriving at Innerleithen, with its flags out.

Innerleithen looked like a working town, a mill town, or maybe a former mill town. We bought pasties in a baker's (I had to train Richard up; it was for his own good), and took them to the town park to sit on a bench and eat.

"That downhill was brilliant," Richard said.

"Worth the climb."

We lounged a bit after we had eaten, resting, but the day was cloudy and cool, so not really lounging weather.

"Shall we press on?" I asked.

"Yeh, I'm OK to."

"Rich, I fancy stopping at Abbotsford."

Abbotsford had been the home of Sir Walter Scott. I'd been vaguely aware of him as the author of 'Ivanhoe', but when I read a bit more before my ride, I found that he had been an almost legendary figure himself. It was not just that his books, such as Waverley and Rob Roy, were hugely popular, but that he had almost reinvented the image of Scotland.

He was writing as memories of the real Jacobite rebellion and Culloden were fading, and as the Clearances were lurching to an end. The image of the clans amongst lowland Scots and the English was still that of backward peasants, and suspicion of them was widespread. Tartan was still banned and the bagpipes were still outlawed; Gaelic was being actively stamped out wherever it could be, and the clans were scattered to America, Australia, England and the slums of the ship-building Clyde and Glasgow.

As Walter Scott wrote romantic tales of the highlands, of honourable clansmen supporting Bonnie Prince Charlie, the mood of the reading classes swung. Scotland's nobility – even a young Queen Victoria herself – claimed the highland clan heritage for themselves. New tartans were woven, bright reds and blues for each clan; and new clan costumes were designed, outlandish costumes claimed as ancient.

Victoria and Prince Albert came north to a magnificent reception in Edinburgh, and were met by the nobles of Scotland in their new 'ancient' finery. She fell under the spell of a romantic highlands which was completely out of touch with real life after the Clearances. The spell lasted, and much later, with Albert's death, it was in the highlands that she hid herself away, in Balmoral, east of the route I had cycled through. Her stay there only reinforced the romantic image of the clans.

Through the 20th century, the cleansed highland culture of tartan and bagpipes and the Prince from Over the Water became the image to the world of the whole of Scotland. Even here in the borders, where the bloodlines are not Celtic, but mostly run back to Anglo-Saxons, Normans and Danes.

"They probably have a café," I said, "at Abbotsford."

"Fine by me."

Our route turned east, shadowing a river which my map told me was the Tweed, and this was another landmark. Before the Piper's Grave I had crossed my last watershed on the way from the far north of Scotland to the border.

The lane hugged the side of the valley, rising and dipping. A lichen-mottled, dry-stone wall lined the road, with the pinky-lilac bells of foxgloves poking up from behind. Grass- and thistle-filled fields dropped away to the river, which meandered through copses and steadily lowering hills.

It was a fantastic road, and so I was disappointed and a little alarmed when it took a sudden turn, crossed the river and deposited us on a main road. We had two miles to negotiate, and it wasn't pleasant. The road ran under dark trees and wasn't really wide enough for cars to overtake bikes with traffic coming the other way. Unfortunately, that wasn't stopping them. Time and again a wing-mirror flashed past.

"Rich," I shouted behind me, "this is horrid. Take care won't you."

I wasn't sure if he heard me, but just took a quick glance over my shoulder every now and then to make sure he was still with me.

It was a real relief when our Route 1 signs took us off the main road, and we pulled in to get our breath and to let our hearts get back to normal.

"Chocolate biscuit?" I asked. "Drink?"

There was no need to ask, really.

It was a steep pull up the side of the valley, but the road was a quiet tree-lined lane, and I was able to meander up to the top. Richard waited for me.

After a couple of miles we were dropping down again into the valley, crossing the main road to a lane running alongside a broadening River Tweed. I studied the map. We were on the wrong side for Abbotsford.

A man was standing proprietarily by a sign advertising the availability of fishing. I guess we didn't look very much like potential angling customers, and he happily told us we could get back up to the main road and cross the river further on.

The main road was broader than before, with cars taking a wider berth around us and it was an easy couple of miles before we were leaving our bikes in the car park for Abbotsford and wandering down a garden path to what seemed like the tradesman's entrance. There was a small queue of elderly visitors, and then us.

The lady selling tickets looked at me with a fixed expression. She probably didn't have many visitors in bright blue Lycra bike shirts.

"Do you have a café?" I asked.

"Yes. At the end of the tour."

"Can we go at the start of the tour?"

The café was the old servants' quarters, under the main rooms.

"You don't," I asked, "have lemon drizzle cake, do you?"

"Sorry."

It had been worth a try, but I decided that must be the end. I would have to live with vitamin deficiency, rickets, scurvy and all the other ailments caused by an extreme lack of lemon drizzle cake. There would be no more requests, no more scanning of menus.

"A scone, please."

We mooched through Sir Walter Scott's library of leather-bound novels and texts into a tall room whose walls held a collection of knives, swords and guns. There were labels such as 'Rob Roy's Dirk' and '16th century Executioner's Sword'. Another room had spears, a chest-plate from Waterloo with a hole where a man's heart would be, and more antlers than you could throw hooplas over.

A door led out to lawns, and looking back, it was a bigger building than I had expected. Built of stone, three storeys high with little turrets at roof level, it was almost a mock Scottish castle, built for the author of romantic Scotland.

My own Scott and Richard's apparently un-named bike carried us the few miles into the town of Melrose and we followed signs for the Youth Hostel past the ruins of the once-great (before the English got to it) Melrose Abbey.

The hostel was an imposing building, tall with large windows looking across a gravelled drive, and steps leading up to a front door and a closed reception desk. Two older ladies were sitting either side of the reception desk waiting for it to open, neither talking to the other. I said hello to both. They didn't say hello to each other.

The hostel warden checked us all in, and handed over bike-shed keys to me.

We walked into the town in search of food to cook, and it was a handsome little place. The market square had been done up, with new seating of coloured sandstone. There were prosperous-looking hotels and some designer shops. It had a nice, if quiet, atmosphere. There was also a Spar and Co-op, from which we emerged with chill-counter curries for the evening, and new supplies of chocolate biscuits for our final day.

The two ladies were both cooking in the large kitchen when we returned. One was preparing a mixed salad; the other was making a rather splendid-looking stirfry, its sizzling odours carrying across to the microwave we were both studying, our curries sitting accusingly in their plastic wrappings and cardboard boxes.

I punctured plastic, put a box in the machine and pressed a variety of buttons in a random order.

Nothing happened.

"Rich, this is ridiculous. How does this thing work?"

I glanced across to the stir-fry lady, who was trying unsuccessfully to suppress a smile.

Richard pressed more buttons, equally randomly.

Nothing happened.

"Tell you what," I said, "I'll do the drinks. This is obviously a task for someone of your age and ability."

"Thanks."

The salad lady was finishing slicing a tomato, and smiled at me.

There was more button-pressing behind me, and then a satisfying hum.

"This works," Richard called across to me at the sink. "If you press the FISH button three times, it starts the five minute timer."

Both ladies were grinning.

"I knew he could do it," I said. "I've taught him well."

Captain's log: Day Fourteen

Target:	39.0 miles	62.4 Km
Actual distance:	48.4 miles	77.4 Km
Average speed:	10.8 mph	17.3 Kmph
Maximum speed:	31.0 mph	49.6 Kmph
Total distance:	597.3 miles	955.6 Km
	Almost 600 miles!	
	Almost 1,000 kilometres!	
	Well now, that was a long way.	

We went out for a walk after our delicious repast (I exaggerate), down past the ruins again, following signs for the Tweed. A grand footbridge led across the river – a suspension bridge, with little towers at either end and a long walkway held by cables. We stood in the middle looking down at a river much wider now than when we were in the hills, and which had lost its youthful exuberance and was flowing more sedately towards the North Sea.

As we walked back off the bridge, I stopped for a last look at the hills on the far side.

Richard carried on, and called back to me, his voice indistinct, "There's a good sign. 'Persons are requested not to cross the bridge in a heavy gale'. 'No loitering, climbing or intentional swinging of the bridge'. 'Only light cabbages'."

I couldn't make out that last word. It couldn't really be cabbages. "Light what?"

"Caaats," he shouted. "No heavy caaats."

I walked across to join him.

He said, "If you do any of those you get a £2 fine or imprisonment. In fact, I think you were loitering just then."

"At least I didn't have any heavy cats."

"Carts," he said. "Carriages."

I looked at him. "Not heavy cats? Or cabbages."

"No," he said. "Not heavy cats. Or cabbages."

Day Fifteen

Target: 45 miles / 72 Km
From Melrose to Berwick-upon-Tweed
via Kelso and the Border

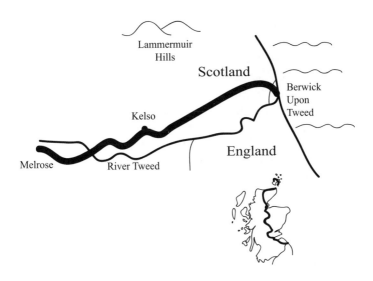

We got lost cycling out of Melrose.

"Do you always get lost?" Richard asked.

"I usually blame Scott."

We had got up early (for us), breakfasted on muesli bars and fruit, said goodbye – separately – to the two ladies eating at opposite ends of the dining room, and cycled into the town centre to look for Route 1 signs.

"There aren't any Route 1 signs," I said.

We tried different exits from the market square, but none of them had a sign.

"Do you think we should look at the map?" Richard asked.

"You're as bad as Scott."

Eventually we found what must have been the original main road, white lines still visible, but grass encroaching from the verges. The road rose steadily up the side of the valley, which was disappointing first thing in the morning; my legs were far from ready for anything involving PWR.

There was a reward for the climb – the Rhymer's Stone, marked by information boards at the side of the road. Legend had it that the Rhymer of Melrose had spoken to the faeries just here, and then disappeared for seven years. When he returned from the land of the faeries, he was said to have supernatural powers and to be able predict the future. He evidently prophesied the battle of Bannockburn and the union of Scotland with England, amongst other events, and his prophesies were consulted by the Jacobites in an attempt to see whether they could win or not.

The sun was a weak reminder of proper summer, as we dropped into Newtown St Boswells and an incongruous set of traffic lights for such a small place.

Claire and I had stayed near here in a holiday cottage before we had children. During the night, I had been vaguely aware of Claire setting off for the loo, only to be woken by a scream. By the time I had reached the bathroom, the light was on and Claire was pointing at a frog in the toilet.

"I felt something hit my bum when I sat down."

"That would be when you screamed."

"It was a bit of a shock."

We stared at the frog for some while, not really sure what to do.

"It must have come from below," I said.

"How?"

"Well, I don't know. But it must have."

I put the lid down on the toilet and – it may have been wrong, very wrong – flushed the loo.

"Don't – "

It was too late.

I opened the lid; it had gone.

"You flushed the toilet."

"It came up. Therefore it could go back down."

Claire had a face for which the word 'aghast' had probably been coined.

I told Richard the story of The Frog in the Bog. He understood. I think it's a man thing.

"My legs are tired," I said.

I looked at the bike computer. We had cycled two and a half miles.

"How far do we have to go today?" Richard asked.

"45 miles. And our train goes at 3.15."

"Right."

We crossed over the Tweed at Dryburgh, home of another of the rich abbeys that had been burned to the ground by the English, another set of giant ruins. Then there was a steep hill up through woods on to a rolling plateau above the level of the river. We joined a quiet B-road, which kept to the high ground, with long views into the distance of pale green fields split by darker hedges and dots of woodland. The grass was lush and long, sprinkled with white wild flowers. I'd no idea what they were called.

I'd been a bit useless at the Nature really. If I did it again, I'd do more Nature. And Whisky. Definitely more Whisky.

Perhaps I could do a cycling tour of Scotland taking in all the whisky distilleries. Although I wasn't sure how that would affect my viewing of Nature.

Away to the south was a suggestion of dark hills, and I wondered if those were the Pennines. England. The end. I wasn't sure I wanted it to end.

Route 1 signs took us off the B-road and we zig-zagged pleasantly for a while, if a little pointlessly, before the signs brought us back to the B-road.

I was starting to feel like brunch now. The bike computer was showing a more respectable twelve miles, and something substantial was needed.

On our right was a high wall, with Floors Castle somewhere behind. We knew it was Floors Castle because a road sign showed $1^{1/2}$ miles to Floors Castle Entrance. The high wall seemed to go on and on, accompanying us as we joined a main road and dropped into Kelso. There were some mighty grounds to Floors Castle.

Kelso was a very different town to Melrose, traditional and no-nonsense, with gentlemen's outfitters, purveyors of fine knitwear and probably ironmongers from whom you could still buy a single nail. A Saturday morning farmer's market was in full swing in the large town square. It was busy and cheery, with cheeses and vegetables and meat and flowers, each stall with a colourful awning of blue-and-white, red-and-white or green-and-white stripes. Flags were stretched between high poles, and a temporary stage was set up at the back.

We strolled around the stalls, buying ourselves sausage rolls flavoured with red onion and cranberries. They were delicious, and we sat on the stage to eat them.

I hadn't noticed while we were wandering that the sky had darkened.

"Did you feel some spots of rain?" Richard asked, as we headed for some bakers to get sandwiches for later.

"It doesn't look like it'll do much," I said. That was

something I wouldn't do on my next ride. Optimism.

We got lost cycling out of Kelso.

Richard blamed me.

"There must have been a sign missing," I said. "Back there, there should have been a sign."

We had joined a main road, only stopping when we realised we were about to go back past Floors Castle.

We turned round and cycled back the way we had come, finding a Route 1 sign that led us towards the coast, rather than in the general direction of Edinburgh and Inverness.

The drizzle was becoming heavierer, the clouds lower, but at least we were back on our quiet B-road, with just the odd car or van sailing past us as we climbed out of Kelso.

A Route 1 sign pointed away from our lovely B-road, and I consulted the map, which was unusual for me.

"Rich," I said, "that's another detour. It just joins up to this road again. And when it does, it goes off again on another diversion. These are just big zig-zags."

The more we looked, the more it seemed daft to leave the B-road, which headed almost plumb-straight for Berwick, wide-ish, with virtually no traffic.

There was another reason for not taking the diversions. One of them would have taken us across the river into England at Norham, and then popped us back north again into Scotland, before the final push into Berwick. Whereas, if we carried straight on, we would reach the border at exactly the point where I had crossed it on my English journey, south to north, two years before. Then, as well, Richard had been with me for the last two days of the journey. There was a symmetry here that felt right.

So we pushed on, still through drizzle. Enough drizzle to have our jackets on, and for our legs, shorts and trainers to be pretty damp. Even so, it was pleasant cycling, gentle ups and downs past fields of grain, tiny hamlets and occasional farms. We chatted, and I told him about my journey.

"How was Scott?" he asked.

I thought about it. He'd been my alter ego, complaining, blaming, moaning. But he'd had no break-downs and not even a puncture, and his Kevlar-lined tyres had given me a certain confidence.

"He's been," I said, "a bit Scott-ish."

"Scottish?"

"No. Scott-*ish*."

"Ah."

As we rode on, I wondered how I had been. If I had cycled the length of Scotland for The Challenge, I had completed it. In fact, I had originally planned a route that was to be 524 miles (838 kilometres) long, but somehow I had clocked up over 600 miles (1,000 kilometres). The difference was no doubt partly from detours, but getting lost so often had probably contributed.

If my journey had been about seeing Scotland's history, then I'd seen quite a bit in fifteen days. Culloden and the Clearances Museum in Bettyhill stuck most in my mind, though there was more, much more that I hadn't seen.

And The Nature? Not a complete success, I was prepared to admit. The ticks in my imaginary I-Spy Scotland book against capercaillies and golden eagles were, shall we say, arguable. I had definitely seen dolphins. And deer. But really, I would have to come back.

Another task had come on me during the journey – a quest to purchase a miniature bottle of whisky at every distillery. This was clearly a failure. Two did not constitute success. And again, I would most certainly have to come back.

Then there was the Mid-Life Crisis. Cycling across England previously had not provided a total cure, and I couldn't be certain about this one. There was, though, something about a long cycle-ride that soothed the mind. It gave a simple target each day – getting to the end. Nothing complicated. Just that simple task. Turn the pedals. Climb the hill. Look at the view. Coast down the far side. Issues and worries were not solved, but somehow moved into the background. There developed a simplicity to life in the saddle. So maybe –

"Scott," I said, "I am considering whether I am cured of Mid-Life Crisis."

"Pardon?" Richard said.

"I was just asking Scott if I am now cured of Mid-Life Crisis."

"What did he say?"

"You interrupted him."

Then again, I thought, perhaps it was none of the above. Perhaps it had been about getting on a bike and cycling. Perhaps it had really been about The Adventure. And perhaps, one day not too far off, I would do it again.

We stopped to eat our sandwiches at Swinton. A bench next to the village football pitch was partly sheltered by a tree, so we sat there eating and taking in the village. The road ran down one side of the pitch, with the other three sides bounded by low stone cottages and houses, with cars and vans parked outside. The people of Swinton would have grandstand views of the action on the pitch from their living room windows. In fact, the odd ball might even make it through living room windows.

It was a good size pitch, exactly fitting the space available. At each end stood, not too surprisingly, goal posts. More surprisingly, where the centre spot ought to be, stood a large stone market cross. It was probably three metres high, a stepped plinth with a column, and on top of that what looked like a large stone sugar lump.

"Can you imagine," I asked my football-playing son, "arriving with an away team and finding that in the middle of the pitch?"

"Where would you kick off?"

"I'm not sure, but you could hide behind it and beat the off-side trap."

"Perhaps they play one-twos off it."

The rain came down harder as we finished our

sandwiches off, and we both put on full waterproofs for the last leg, the final push.

Our road now had more gentle downs than gentle ups, and the signposts counted down the miles to Berwick-upon-Tweed. With about six miles to go, Route 1 re-joined our B-road, and it was nice to see it back. I'd been on Route 1 round Orkney and down to Inverness, and it was a good way to finish.

Then there was a deep dip in the road that I recognised from two years before, a down-and-up that generally a cyclist would head into fast, so that the momentum carries you up the other side.

I stopped, and Richard pulled in beside me.

"Rich, this is it!"

"What?"

"The border. Look."

The back of a large sign was facing us, and I knew what was on the other side. We freewheeled down to the sign and turned to face it, reading the large letters against the brown background:

SCOTLAND
WELCOMES YOU

Richard had the most enormous grin on his face. There's a possibility I did as well.

"Scott," I said. "We've made it." I patted his handle-bars.

"Well done, Dad," Richard said.

"Thanks. And thanks for coming."

"It's been brilliant."

"We're not quite there yet. Come on. Here we go."

I pushed off.

"YEEHAAAA!"

Behind me I heard, "WOOHOOOO!"

We picked up speed, hit the bottom of the dip and pedalled madly up the other side, finding ourselves flashing past a smaller white sign, and we were now officially in England.

I stopped and looked back. Scotland still welcomed me.

We cycled on the last few miles, dropping down into Berwick-upon-Tweed itself, half-remembering the route from last time. Into the town centre, and out again in search of the sea.

We came out under the massive ramparts that fortify the town. We cycled alongside each other, ramparts on one side, pebble-strewn beach and tidal mud-flats leading out to the grey waters of the estuary of the Tweed.

"I don't think Scott will fancy me hauling him across all that mud to dip his front wheel in the water."

"I don't fancy it myself."

I said, "I know a good place to finish."

A long pier stood guard over the harbour and the estuary, with its sand-bars, ripples and wavelets. Concrete and functional. No tourist attraction. But at the far end stood a low red-and-white lighthouse.

We pedalled out along the pier, stopping at the very end.

South was England, North was Scotland, and beyond the lighthouse stretched a wide, wide sea.

Captain's log: Day Fifteen

Target:	45.0 miles	72.0 Km
Actual distance:	45.3 miles	72.5 Km
Average speed:	11.9 mph	19.0 Kmph
Maximum speed:	31.0 mph	49.6 Kmph

We found a café in Berwick. I checked down the menu.

Carrot cake.

Fruit scone.

Pineapple upside down cake.

Fine sources of vitamins, no doubt, but my eyes lit on the true quest of my journey.

I guess Scott noticed a spring in my step when I came out. Perhaps a steadier eye. My hair glossier. That sort of thing.

"Lemon drizzle cake?" he said.

"Oh, yes."

Captain's log: The whole journey

Total target distance: **524.0 miles**   **838.4 Km**

Total actual distance: **642.6 miles**   **1028.1 Km**

Ending

We had been home a week or two. I was in the bar of a hotel, fully intending to order a pint of something hand-pulled in a straight glass. My eyes fastened on the rows of bottles of amber liquid on the shelves behind.

There must have been a hundred or so there. I read each label, working my way across. There was Scapa and Highland Park from Orkney; Glenmorangie, made by the Sixteen Men of Tain in Sutherland; Tomatin and Dalwhinnie from the Cairngorms; Ardbeg, made on Islay, but taking me back to the American with the hip flask at Newtonmore; Blair Athol and Edradour as the road finally came out of the mountains, and Glenkinchie that I had bypassed as I rode south from Edinburgh. It was like my journey through Scotland passing in front of me, each one prompting a memory.

I could quite easily have ordered one of each.

I didn't though.

After all, I thought, it's a good excuse to go back.

Acknowledgements

I consulted or mentioned various books, maps and websites for my journey, some clearly more than others:

The Complete Book of British Birds, published by The Automobile Association and The Royal Society of British Birds, 1988. (This was more of a flick-through than a consultation.)

Michael Jackson's Malt Whisky Companion, Dorling Kindersley, 2004. (This was more of a consultation than a flick-through.)

The Lion in the North: One Thousand Years of Scottish History, by John Prebble, Penguin, 1981.

The Life and Times of the Black Pig – A biography of Ben Macdui, by Ronald Turnbull, published by Millrace, 2007. (The source for the legend of The Grey Man.)

Waverley, by Sir Walter Scott, Oxford University Press, 1986. (Originally published in 1814.)

Lochs & Glens Cycleway Guide Book, by Fergal MacErlean, Sustrans/Pocket Mountains, 2007.

www.undiscoveredscotland.co.uk. (This was useful – information on each town.)

I-Spy Nature in Scotland. (This is a fib. I haven't got this one. In fact, I don't think it exists, though perhaps it should.)

and *The Full English, by Mike Carden, Bike Ride Books, 2007.* (You'll like this one.)

Maps & Routes

In order of usage, north to south, these are the main Sustrans National Cycle Network maps I used for my route:

Route 1: Aberdeen to John O'Groats

Route 7: Lochs & Glens North, Glasgow to Inverness

Route 77: The Salmon Run, Dundee to Pitlochry

Route 1: Coast & Castles North, Edinburgh to Aberdeen

Route 1: Coast & Castles South, Edinburgh to Newcastle upon Tyne

The maps and routes do change over time; up-to-date ones are usually available at the Rannerdale Cycle Maps website.

The following are organisations that can be useful for a long-distance cycle ride:

CTC – the national cycling organisation

Sustrans – the charity which builds many of the cycle routes in the UK

The Scottish Youth Hostel Association and the Youth Hostel Association

Links to them can be found on the Bike Ride Books website

www.bikeridebooks.co.uk

Advanced Paranoia

Some names in the text have been changed
to protect the innocent, with their voices digitally
altered, their tummies tucked and their faces botox'd.
So if you think you recognise yourself, you don't;
any similarity to anybody ever is entirely coincidental,
and is purely a result of advanced paranoia –
probably mine.

Thanks

Thanks so much to all those who have encouraged
me to write this, or have helped in its production:
Claire, Lisa, Suzie, and Richard,
my brother Andy, Richard Peace,
Megan Taylor, Viv Hamnett,
Margaret & Ian Pollard, Dave Freeborn,
Robin Grenville-Evans for his wonderful illustrations
and slightly reluctantly

Scott
without whom...

My Dad died in between the cycling of Scotland
and the writing of the book. I miss him,
and this book is dedicated to him:

Robert Henry Carden.
A gentle man,
in every sense.

Also by Mike Carden

The Full English

"Mike's relaxed and chatty style is never less than entertaining, making The Full English the sort of book that can put a smile on your face even when it is cold, grey Winter outside."
Dorset County Magazine

"A great read. A lightening guide to the country with simple un-heroic endeavour and humour."
Velo Vision

"A joyful read that will sweep away the dark nights of winter and conjure up memories of summer days in the countryside."
www.TheHistoryMagazine.co.uk

"Warm, well observed, unpretentious and very funny."
Adventure Travel

"England's answer to Round Ireland with a Fridge – but without the fridge."
Ludlow Advertiser

"9/10. A delightfully individual account of tripping the length of England by bike."
Cycling Plus

"An easily read book, humorous, well written and full of the eccentricities of the English."
Arrivée